Enlightened Women

'This is a brave and intellectually rigorous book, which goes against the grain of current orthodoxies to challenge some of the postmodern assumptions in the interest of a political project – feminism – that we should not discard.'

Elizabeth Wilson

Over the last few years, postmodern feminist theory has itself become academic orthodoxy. The humanist subject is dead, there is no objective reality, and those who use the category 'woman' collude in oppressive discursive practices – positions like these are by now part of the postmodern mainstream. With *Enlightened Women* Alison Assiter mounts a radical critique of this wholesale rejection of Enlightenment thought.

In the opening chapters of her book, Assiter provides a lucid exposition of contemporary postmodern feminism. She analyses the writings of some of its most influential theorists, and places them in the wider context of postmodern and post-structuralist theory as developed, for example, by Lyotard and Derrida. Assiter then develops a critique of the antirealist stance that unites postmodern thinkers and makes a powerful argument for epistemological realism.

In later chapters, Assiter goes on to outline a 'modernist' feminist epistemology based on communities rather than the individual; she asserts that a version of the humanist subject based on bodily identity can be defended against postmodernist deconstructions; and she demonstrates that we can indeed make claims about women that are universally true. *Enlightened Women* argues for retaining the distinction between sex and gender and concludes with an alternative reading of the theory of sexuality.

Enlightened Women provides a clear and concise overview of postmodernism and French feminist thought; at the same time it argues, against received opinion, for a partial return to modernist values.

Alison Assiter is Head of Social Studies at the University of Luton. She is the author of *Althusser and Feminism* and *Pornography, Feminism and the Individual* as well as co-editor of *Bad Girls, Dirty Pictures*.

Enlightened Women

Modernist Feminism in a Postmodern Age

Alison Assiter

London and New York

First published 1996
by Routledge
11 New Fetter Lane, London EC4P 4EE

Simultaneously published in the USA and Canada
by Routledge
29 West 35th Street, New York, NY 10001

© 1996 Alison Assiter

Typeset in Sabon by Florencetype Ltd, Stoodleigh, Devon

Printed and bound in Great Britain by Clays Ltd, St Ives plc

British Library Cataloguing in Publication Data
A catalogue record for this book is available from the British Library.

Library of Congress Cataloging in Publication Data
A catalogue record for this book has been requested.

ISBN 0–415–08338–9 (hbk)
ISBN 0–415–08339–7 (pbk)

To the memory of my beloved mother, who died, in October 1994, after many years of suffering; and to Ben's wonderful new 'surrogate' grandmother, Ga-Ga or Pamela.

Contents

Acknowledgements

I would like to thank the various people who have commented on sections of the manuscript, including: Keith Graham, Chris Cherry, Cordelia Bryan, Morwenna Griffiths, Phyllis Creme, Kathy Lennon, Margaret Whitford, Kate Soper and Gill Hague. I would like to acknowledge the help of the Women and Philosophy group, both in encouraging me to continue with the text, and in providing constructive criticism. I am especially grateful, in addition to the women already mentioned, to Susan Khin Zaw, Anne Seller, Christine Battersby, and Mina Dandha. I would also like to acknowledge the help of an unknown American reader who, through her detailed reader's reports, helped me track down some of the mistakes, typos, spelling errors and misquotations in earlier drafts. I owe a particular debt to Alan Haworth, who went through the entire manuscript locating the misspellings and the typos. He couldn't resist some commentary on the argument as well. I must thank Cyril for heeding Ben's shouts when my head was buried in my text; and Caroline Hinch for typing out sections of the text that were written in my dreadful longhand, in trains, on the beach on holiday and at 2.00 am. I should also like to thank Tina Chanter for encouraging me to take Derrida seriously. Finally, I must thank Sarah Cahill, who copy-edited the manuscript, and who really exceeded the duties of a copy-editor as she tracked down most of the remaining biographical and other errors.

I cannot acknowledge any foundation, for I did not receive one, nor have I ever had a sabbatical. But I would like to thank God, or whoever it was, who gave me flu, at just the point when the final corrections on the script were due. Seriously, I have never particularly enjoyed the role of the full-time researcher, and I have completed this manuscript while carrying out quite a demanding job directing a project at North London University that is designed to increase equality of career opportunity.

x   Acknowledgements

This and my limitations mean that there remain many errors in the text. I hope that others will find something of interest in it, and that they will continue the work where I have left questions unanswered or arguments only partially developed.

Earlier versions of Chapters 2 and 3 appeared in my book *Althusser and Feminism*, Pluto Press, 1990; and an earlier version of Chapter 8 appeared in *Bad Girls, Dirty Pictures*, ed. A. Assiter and A. Carol, Pluto Press, 1993.

Introduction

Postmodernism: The Background

In 1987, one of the central protagonists of 'postmodernism' had this to say:

> Fastidious academics once shunned the word *postmodern* as they might shrink from the shadiest neologism. But now the term has become a shibboleth for tendencies in film, theatre, dance, music, art and architecture; in philosophy, theology, psychoanalysis and historiography; in new sciences, cybernetic technologies, and various cultural lifestyles. Indeed, postmodernism has now received the bureaucratic accolade of the National Endowment for the Humanities in the form of Summer Seminars for College Teachers; and beyond that, it has penetrated the discourse of late Marxist critics who, only a decade ago, dismissed the term as another instance of the dreck, fads and folderol of a consumer society.[1]

'Postmodernism' was propelled into the limelight by changes in architecture and the arts. In its early forms, it is associated with changes in the architectural domain. Commentators refer to the attempts of architects to distance themselves from the 'modern', 'concrete slab' style of architects like Corbusier. Modernists sought, in the words of Charles Jencks: '[to combine] . . . Modern techniques with something else (usually traditional building) in order for architecture to communicate with the public and a concerned minority, usually other architects'.[2] Postmodernists sought to democratise architectural techniques; to make architecture more available and acceptable. The expression 'postmodernist' is extended to apply to other art forms, including literature. Experts differ both on who is a

1

postmodernist – Joyce, for example, is a modernist for Jameson and a postmodernist for Lyotard[3] – what it is and when it began; some affirm, indeed, that these questions stem from a way of thinking that 'questions the validity of such dichotomous thought patterns'.[4] Correlatively, any attempt to define the phenomenon is seen to be self-defeating, since to do so would be to posit a unity, a presence, which postmodernists occlude.

Yet, a number of attempts have been made to say what postmodernism is. Andreas Huyssen, for example, sketches 'four major characteristics' of 'the early phase of postmodernism': a period he identifies as occurring in the 1960s, predominantly in the USA. First, he suggests, postmodernism was characterised by 'a temporal imagination which displayed a powerful sense of the future and of new frontiers, of rupture and discontinuity, of crisis and generational conflict, an imagination reminiscent of earlier continental avant garde movements such as Dada and surrealism'.[5] Second, the early phase of postmodernism included an iconoclastic attack on what Peter Burger has tried to capture theoretically as 'institution art'.[6] Institution art, he argues, served to support a cultural establishment and its claims to aesthetic knowledge. Against this, postmodernists advocated pop, psychedelic art, acid rock, alternative and street theatre, focusing on mass culture as against 'high' art.

Huyssen's third characteristic of 1960s postmodernism is a 'technological optimism':[7] Mcluhan's cybernetic and media eschatology 'all combined easily with euphoric visions of a postindustrial society'.[8] Finally, postmodernism, Huyssen suggests, heralded a wider reaction against 'modern' society: 'postmodernism harboured the promise of a "post male", "post white", "post humanist" and "post puritan" world'.[9]

According to Arthur Kroker and David Cooke: 'Ours is a fin-de-millennium consciousness'.[10] Others refer to the contemporary world as a 'postindustrial' society: a 'world' that is essentially at odds with the industrial capitalist reality that Marx, to take but one figure, described. Many 'postmodernists', indeed, characterise the view as offering a designation of a particular cultural epoch – the age of late capitalism – whilst they simultaneously question the legitimacy and possibility of referring to 'epochs' at all. Leslie Fiedler, for example, in 'Cross the Border – Close the Gap',[11] describes 'another time' that we've entered: 'apocalyptic, antirational, blatantly romantic and sentimental'. For him, the 'birth pangs' of postmodernism occurred in the mid-1950s, with the emergence of Pop Art and 1950s American novels and films. Postmodernist society is Irving Howe's 'mass society' – 'a world increasingly shapeless and an experience increasingly fluid'[12] – the world of the 1950s British angry young men (John Osborne and Kingsley Amis) and the San Francisco 'beat' novelists.

Lyotard, the postmodern thinker *par excellence*, (he is one of the few writers actually to use the term), questions the 'grand narratives of legitimation'. Traditionally, he argues, science has always been in conflict with narratives; for postmodernists, by contrast, all knowledge is a kind of narrative, a kind of language game. 'Grand narratives' are overarching theories of history which suggest a progressive improvement in the human condition. Condorcet's 'Sketch of the Progress of the Human Mind' pinpoints the notion. Progress is anathema to Lyotard: 'the idea of progress as possible was rooted in the certainty that the development of the arts, technology, knowledge and liberty would be profitable to mankind as a whole'.[13] After two centuries (since the Enlightenment), Lyotard suggests, it is no longer possible to believe that. Overarching philosophies of history, such as the Enlightenment belief in the progress of reason and liberty, Hegel's dialectic, and, notably, Marx's theory of the progressive development of the productive forces, are no longer credible. Since these theories are about emancipation and the overcoming of inequalities, a postmodern rejection of such theories suggests the loss of the possibility of emancipation.

Postmodernism and Poststructuralism

Recent postmodernist influenced writing has been informed by 'post-structuralist' theory. Poststructuralism grew out of the structuralist writing of Saussure, Althusser and Lévi-Strauss. Structuralism is a methodology of the human sciences; it is associated with a particular reading of Saussure's *Course in General Linguistics*. Saussure provides a model of language as a system all of whose parts are interrelated. Following Saussure, structuralist thinkers focus on synchronic analysis of phenomena, and they challenge the assumption that the history of metaphysics is the history of the gradually growing self-empowerment of subjectivity.

For theorists like Jacques Lacan, Jacques Derrida and Michel Foucault, structuralism has not moved sufficiently far from metaphysics. Broadly, poststructuralists not only deny the possibility of objective knowledge of an independently existing real world, but they stress the potentially manipulative powers of 'discourses' which have attained the status of knowledge. Not only do they doubt whether there can be any discourse called 'science' which is intrinsically different from other 'narratives' but they assert the instrumental rationality of what has been called 'science' and the military and ecological catastrophes into which pursuit of 'science' has led us. Overall, then, poststructuralists have challenged the liberal humanist rhetoric; its 'universalising' theorising about the human subject, and the values to which it appeals. The liberal humanist subject is said to be a construction of certain 'discourses' which have tended to consign marginalised 'subjects' like women to object status. The poststructuralist subject, by contrast, is decentred and fragmented. The values, furthermore, on which liberal humanist theory depends, have been argued to be themselves tainted by the discursive practices in which they are bound up. Some poststructuralist theory, then, goes further than the assertion of a relativism of value to claim that it is not possible to speak of values like justice or freedom, since these values are tied to oppressive discourses of power.

Poststructuralism has been described as the discourse of postmodernity. The roots of postmodernism[14] can be traced further back to thinkers like Nietzsche and even de Sade. The postmodern condition has been characterised by Jane Flax[15] as involving three features: the deaths of Man, History and Metaphysics. It involves the rejection of so-called 'essentialist' conceptions of human activity: the dismissal of unity and totality. Postmodernists foreground the aesthetic. Some, e.g. Deleuze and Guattari, develop a 'politics of desire': they offer a challenge to subject centred reason, through the body. The Enlightenment ideal of a unified rational subject is replaced by one of 'liberation' by the release of multiple desiring intensities. Desire is seen to be constitutive of social reality.

Postmodernism has, as Kate Soper has put it: 'issued a number of challenges: to the idea that we can continue to think, write and speak of our culture as representing a continuous development and progress, to the idea that we can invoke any universal subjectivity in speaking about the human condition.'[16]

Feminism and Postmodernism

Feminism and postmodernism, in one sense, are natural allies. Feminism, like postmodernism, has developed new paradigms of social criticism. It has uncovered the political power of 'universal' knowledge claims. In the 1970s, feminists argued that many assertions that are put forward as universally true are only true for men. Later feminists extended this to argue that the claims are often only true for men of a particular culture, class and race. Feminist philosophers have gone further to suggest that even the ideals of 'objectivity' and 'reason' reflect masculinity in a particular historical period.

Recently, however, there have emerged other reasons for a closer alliance between postmodernism and feminism. Critics of the 'early' writings of the women's movement, such as the work of Shulamith Firestone, Nancy Chodorow and Marxist feminists, argued that their work tended to reflect a perspective that was their own: white, western and middle class. These 'universalising' feminists were, the critics argued, reflecting, in their own work, universalising assumptions of which they were critical in the work of male theorists. Some critics went so far as to argue that this problem arose from their failure to locate their pronouncements in the historical context in which they were writing. Their writing suffered, therefore, these critics argued, from tendencies towards a 'false' objectivity. Postmodernism, with its questioning of 'grand narratives of legiti-mation', to use Lyotard's words, seemed, therefore, for many feminists, to be a natural ally.

More recently still, postmodern feminism has itself come in for quite extensive criticism. Squires, for example, argues for a qualified return to 'principled positions'.[17] Barrett and Phillips suggest that 'in legitimate critique of some of the earlier [feminist] assumptions we may stray too far from feminism's original project.'[18]

At the same time, recent critics of postmodernism have urged that we retain many of its assumptions. Squires suggests, for example, that we need 'a post-Enlightenment defence of principled positions, without the essentialist or transcendental illusions of Enlightenment thought'.[19] I would like to argue in this book, however, that many critics of postmodernism have not yet gone far enough. Kate Soper has argued forcefully that post-modernists implicitly appeal to the very values they are rejecting in claiming their position to be preferable to the one they are criticising. I will go further, and invite a rethinking of a number of the categories – essentialism, the humanist subject, knowledge of an objective reality – that postmodernists are inclined to reject. I concur with Patricia Waugh, when she says: 'feminism cannot sustain itself as an emancipatory movement unless it acknowledges its foundation in the discourses of modernity.'[20]

This book is written partly for undergraduates on Cultural Studies, Women's Studies, Critical Theory, Sociology, Politics and Philosophy programmes. Some sections of it, therefore, deliberately set out to be intro-ductory. The book is also, however, intended to be a contribution to the debate about feminism and postmodernism amongst academics.

I begin the book by looking at the work of three postmodern feminists – Nancy Fraser, Linda Nicholson and Judith Butler – who have invited us to reject essentialist, universalising feminist theories and the category 'woman' as caught up in patrocentric discursive practices. I begin a critique of these themes. I have chosen to begin the book with this work, both because it is particularly influential at the moment, and also because it offers, I believe, a useful summary of debates in postmodern feminism.

Although many would not describe Luce Irigaray as a postmodern thinker, her reformulation of the locus of patterns of discrimination to the domain of the symbolic sets the scene for much feminist postmodern writing. Additionally, she is a very important feminist thinker influenced by poststructuralism. Chapter 2, therefore, outlines some of the influences on her writing and some major themes in her work. It also begins a critique of these themes.

Many recent advocates of postmodernism have been anti-realist, and the assertion that one cannot describe viewpoints as being true or false, or right or wrong, is becoming commonplace. It is sometimes said that all one can do is tell stories, and one chooses the story one likes best. I believe that, in a world in which there are horrendous wars taking place, the environment is being destroyed, and there is mass starvation, this view is morally and politically reprehensible. It stems from the anti-realist position that one cannot make claims about a world which is independent of the speaker. Chapter 3 defends an unfashionable realist approach to meaning, and outlines the anti-realist elements (which may not always be apparent) in some of the most influential thinkers of postmodernity.

Postmodernism is often thought to imply a rejection of the classical humanist subject. Foucault, in his important essay 'What is Enlightenment?', is at pains both to distinguish 'Enlightenment' thinking, as represented mainly by Kant's piece 'An Answer to the Question: What is Enlightenment?',[21] from humanism, and to emphasise that he is not 'rejecting' either. However, some contemporary postmodern thinkers argue both that Enlightenment and humanism are closely linked and that the classical humanist subject is an entity of a bygone age. In this argument, in the feminist context, Irigaray is a philosophical precursor, and I devote a chapter of the book (Chapter 4) to this theme. I argue against a wholesale rejection of the humanist subject. With this chapter I conclude the mainly critical half of the book.

Chapter 5 begins the process of offering a more positive 'modernist' feminism by describing a feminist epistemology which is compatible with the realism defended in Chapter 3. I argue for a version of the view that the subjects of knowledge are communities rather than individuals. Further, I argue that it is the standpoint of the community most committed to 'emancipatory' values that has the greatest claim to epistemic validity. The postmodernist challenge reappears here, in the guise of the sceptic who questions whether one can decide this kind of question at all.

As we have seen, postmodernists have questioned transcendental reason and the possibility of there being any transhistorical, culture independent norms. Some, indeed, have gone so far as to question the possibility of norms at all. In Chapter 6, I defend a notion of practical reason against these criticisms.

Chapter 7 moves on to offer a 'modernist' view in an area that lies at the heart of feminism. Many postmodern feminists have argued that the 'universalising' feminisms of the early part of the second wave feminism are no longer tenable. Postmodernists, influenced by the very important claims made by black women and by lesbian women about many of the false generalisations made about women, have questioned the possibility of any 'universal' claims being made about women at all. In this chapter, I unravel different elements of this postmodern critique, and argue that there is a sense in which one not only can, but also should, uphold 'universal' claims about women.

The final, eighth, chapter is rather different in character from the others.

Instead of falling within the broad philosophical domain of the rest of the book, it covers a particular area of investigation: the theory of sexuality. I make no apologies, however, for its presence in the book, for it is a topic that has received extensive recent coverage, most of it offering a poststructuralist/postmodernist reading of the theory. I offer an alternative reading of the theory of sexuality.

Overall, then, the book advocates a return to 'Enlightenment' values on realism in the theory of meaning, on universalism in feminist theory, and on the value of the cognitive domain. But the particular approaches to these questions taken in the book have been strongly influenced by postmodern critiques.

1
The Flight from Universals

> Here no tendency appeared, on the part of his father's trousers,
> for example, to break up into an arrangement of appearances,
> grey, flaccid and probably fistular or of his father's legs to vanish
> in the farce of their properties, no but his father's legs and
> trousers, as they seem, in the wood, remained legs and trousers.
> (Samuel Beckett, *Watt*)

In the eighteenth century, David Hume offered some famous arguments in
favour of scepticism about knowledge.[1] The only items in which we are justified in claiming to have knowledge, according to Hume, are 'impressions'
and 'ideas'. For the inference from idea to object to be justified, Hume
argued, there must be a necessary connection between the two. But no such
connection can be found. Furthermore, a further necessary condition for
the belief in the existence of objects being rational is that an account should
be provided of the identity of objects. Hume could not do this, so he attributed the belief that objects have an identity to custom and imagination.

Many feminists influenced by postmodernism and poststructuralism
have reached a conclusion about 'women' and about certain types of
feminist theorising that is similar to Hume's view about the identity
of objects. In this first chapter, I would like to look at the work of a
number of recent feminists who have expressed scepticism about the category 'woman', and about 'universalising' 'essentialist' feminist theorising.
This chapter, and the three following, will outline some of my disagreements with certain aspects of postmodern/poststructuralist thinking.

Judith Butler

I'd like to begin by looking at an American writer, whose work *Gender
Trouble*[2] is receiving a good deal of attention in the USA and the

UK. Her book has been hailed as 'finding problematic' the category of 'female'.

Butler sets out to subvert the claim 'that there is some existing identity understood through the category of woman, who not only initiates feminist interests and goals within discourses, but constitutes the subject for whom political representation is pursued' (p. 1). She argues, through a series of very interesting discussions of theories of gender identity, that the category of 'woman' may be a construct produced by the very political system that is supposed to facilitate its emancipation. The idea that there is a subject – woman – 'oppressed' by that of which it is 'the other' – men – is part of the foundationalist fable. The assumption that there is a category of persons – women as a group – is an unacceptable legacy of Enlightenment rationalism. The category 'woman', she suggests, may be a reification of gender relations that are antithetical to feminism.

The focus of Butler's enquiry is to produce a genealogy – after Foucault – of gender ontology. She sets out both to understand the question of the division between the genders, and to deconstruct the idea that gender is a substantive category.

Butler's work fits one central 'postmodern', 'poststructuralist' presupposition. This is a claim that derives from Nietzsche, that is pursued in the structuralist writings of Louis Althusser, and is to be found in the work of Foucault, Derrida and Deleuze. The view is that the individual self is a fiction – it is an historically contingent construct. Butler readily acknowledges her debt to Nietzsche. She deploys an argument gleaned from Michael Haar on Nietzsche: 'that a number of philosophical ontologies have been trapped within certain illusions of "Being" and "substance" that are fostered by the belief that the grammatical formulation of subject and predicate reflects the prior ontological reality of substance and attribute' (p. 20). According to Haar, says Butler, the critique of the metaphysics of substance implies a rejection of the very notion of the psychological person as a substantive thing. She quotes Haar:

> The destruction of logic by means of its genealogy brings with it as well the ruin of the psychological categories founded upon this logic. All psychological categories (the ego, the individual, the person) derive from the illusion of substantial identity. But this illusion goes back basically to a superstition that deceives not only commonsense but also philosophers – namely, the belief in language and, more precisely, in the truth of grammatical categories. It was grammar (the structure of subject and predicate) that inspired Descartes' certainty that the 'I' is the subject of 'think'. (pp. 20–21)

It would be possible to take a 'modern humanist' stance on the subject, whilst opting for a postmodern perspective on the gendered subject.

However, this would go very much against the grain of Butler's writing. Although the form taken by her version of the critique is very different, it fits with this remark of Foucault:

> The individual is not a pregiven entity which is seized on by the exercise of power. The individual, with his identity and characteristics, is the product of a relation of power exercised over bodies, multiplicities, movements, desire forces.'[3]

Throughout his writings, Foucault discusses the constitution of the self as a subject. The individual, in his view, is 'not the vis-a-vis of power', but 'one of its prime effects'.[4] Butler, too, argues that there is no 'doer behind the deed' but that 'the doer is constructed in and through the deed'. Butler suggests that if the subject 'woman' is a construction of feminism, then identity politics has its limitations. Identity, indeed, may be a normative ideal. Specifically, Butler is interested in the question of the extent to which gender is a heterosexual construct.

It would take a whole book to respond to Butler's challenges. The ensuing chapters of this book, on meaning (Chapter 3), on the self (Chapter 4), and on universalism (Chapter 7), could each be taken to be a partial response to her arguments, although none of them is couched specifically in terms of a direct attempt at an 'answer' to Butler. At this stage, I would like to do no more than raise some questions about Butler's approach, and then I have chosen a particular section of her second chapter – on Freud – to respond to in detail. I have chosen this section because it represents, in my view, a crucial component of her argument to the effect that gender identity may be a heterosexist construct.

For the moment, I would like to raise the following questions about Butler's position: how can one create oneself as a self if there is no antecedently existing self to do the creating? Elsewhere, I have cast doubt on the idea that the notion of responsibility can apply if our individual motivations are beyond our control.[5] How, on Butler's view, can we make sense of the idea that a person could have acted otherwise than they did? Furthermore, if the subject of feminism is a fiction produced by the discourse of feminism, what are we to make of early second wave feminism? Is it to be dismissed as the ravings of a few discursively constructed white, middle class women,[6] or is it a movement that helped sow the seeds for the political flowering of other groupings, however they are categorised? How, indeed, can we ground a feminist politics that deconstructs the female subject? How is Butler's view, in the end, different from the classical liberal view that 'underneath' we are all the same, and that gender is irrelevant to questions of justice or truth?

I will leave these questions for now, and move to look in detail at the section of Butler's text on Freud.

Butler on Freud

In her discussion of Freud's account of gender formation, Butler focuses on two of Freud's essays: 'Mourning and Melancholia' (1917)[7] and 'The Ego and the Id' (1923).[8] In the first of these two essays, Freud considers the phenomena of 'mourning', on the one hand, and 'melancholia' on the other. Mourning, he explains, is a state of mind following the loss of a loved object. In some people, he points out, the same influences produce melancholia instead of mourning (p. 252). Melancholia is distinguished by a 'profoundly painful dejection, cessation of interest in the outside world' (p. 252). Melancholia, for Freud, can sometimes occur when it is not clear what the subject has lost. Melancholics, unlike those in mourning, suffer a loss in self-regard, an 'impoverishment of the ego on a grand scale' (p. 252). Melancholia can be explained, Freud argues, by the person both internalising the lost object – identifying with it – and subjecting this object to abuse and vilification. The ego, in other words, is turned against itself. The ego debases itself and rages against itself.

Freud suggests that this process plays a significant role in determining the form taken by the ego. Butler argues, however, that it is not just the formation of the ego – or 'its character', as Freud calls it – that is being described, but the acquisition of gender identity as well. The intervening strategy of melancholia 'does not *oppose* the work of mourning but may be the only way in which the ego can survive the loss of its essential emotional ties to others' (p. 58 in Butler, *Gender Trouble*). The incest-taboo initiates a loss of a love object for the ego, and the ego overcomes this loss through internalisation of the 'tabooed object of desire'. In the case of a prohibited heterosexual union, she continues, it is the object which is renounced, but not 'the modality of desire' (pp. 58–59). However, where it is a prohibited homosexual union that may be in question, 'it is clear that both the desire and the object require renunciation and so become subject to the internalizing strategies of melancholia' (p. 59).

Freud introduced the Oedipus complex to explain why the boy must repudiate the mother and adopt an ambivalent attitude towards the father. The boy must, according to Freud, repress his love for his mother because of his fear of castration. Butler adds a further dimension, however. She suggests that there is, in Freud's work, an implicit second claim: that there are two ways of desiring an object – a masculine way and a feminine way. Freud, Butler claims, in relying upon the fear of castration (meaning the loss of the penis) as the major threat to which the boy is subject, has suppressed the further possibility, namely, that the boy fears 'castration' in the metaphorical sense of 'feminisation'. If the boy rejects the 'hetero-sexual cathexis' altogether, he is effectively internalising the mother, as the melancholic does, and adopting a feminine 'way' of desiring.

Butler goes on to argue that Freud does not really conceptualise each of us as originally properly bisexual (as he is usually read as doing). What Freud describes as bisexuality is, in fact, a combination of two hetero-sexual desires – the boy desiring the mother and the father (the male and the female 'other') in a heterosexual way. Full bisexuality would involve not only desiring both categories of object, but in the two possible ways.

Butler asks: how could we identify a primary bisexuality? She suggests that, in fact, we cannot distinguish dispositions – masculine or feminine ways of desiring – from internalisations: the parent (the mother for the boy, for example) is not only prohibited as an object of love, but is inter-nalised as a prohibiting or withholding object of love. The ego ideal, then, works to repress or inhibit the expression of desire for that parent. Gender identification, therefore, is a kind of melancholia in which the sex of the prohibited object is internalised as a prohibition. 'This prohibition sanc-tions and regulates discrete gender identity and the law of heterosexual desire' (p. 63).

The description of gender identification as a 'kind of melancholia', however, seems a little strange: as we saw, melancholia, for Freud, involves the internalisation of the lost object, and the simultaneous directing of invective against that object, internalised within the self. Melancholia, in the case in question, would involve the ego turning against the object internalised as a prohibition: the boy's ego, for example, being directed against the mother internalised as a prohibiting agent. What Butler seems to mean, however, is not this, but the internalisation of the prohibition.

Butler points out that not all gender identification is based on the successful implementation of the taboo against homosexuality. Therefore, gender identity as it is constructed is an 'internalisation of a prohibition that is formative of identity'. The identity, indeed, is maintained by the consistent application of the taboo. Thus the language of 'disposition' is not foundational at all, but is rather an effect of the application of the taboo. 'Dispositions' are traces of a history of enforced sexual prohibi-tions. In Foucauldian vein, Butler announces that the illusion of sexuality before the law is a creation of the law.

This is an interesting and unusual reading of Freud. There are some factors, however, that Butler leaves out of her picture. Sexuality, for Freud, is primarily and initially not bisexual – there is no primary bisexual dispo-sition – but 'polymorphously perverse'. It is directed on anything and everything – the thumb, the breast, the dummy, the bottle, and so on.

It is questionable, indeed, whether Freud posits a 'foundational' sexu-ality at all. There is certainly nothing in his theory which is 'foundational' in the sense that it is a 'metatheory' grounding the truth of the theory of sexuality. The 'foundation' could not be itself a component of his theory of sexuality if it were to perform this role. There is, therefore, no logical or epistemological 'foundation' in Freud's theory.

There are facets of Freud's theory which are 'foundational' in a much weaker second sense: these aspects develop before anything else in the 'progression' of a child's sexual life. But it is the 'polymorphously perverse' drives which are foundational in this sense. In *Three Essays on Sexuality*,[9] Freud suggests that heterosexuality has to be explained and not assumed, and that boys and girls are bisexual at an early stage of their development. However, bisexuality is not temporally foundational. Butler, perhaps, has a third sense of foundationalism in mind: bisexual dispositions are hypostatised by Freud to be 'foundational' in the acquisition of a sense of self and gender identity in that they occur earlier (though not before anything else) and they are logically required by the latter. They are logically prior in that gender identity could not happen without them, and they precede the formation of gender in fact. It seems that it is this thesis that Butler sets out to question and subvert. She claims that it is subverted because the Freudian conception of bisexuality is overlaid by his heterosexual predisposition. Freud is not positing true bisexuality – the girl desiring the mother in a feminine way and the father in a masculine way – because Freud unconsciously reads these desires through a heterosexual matrix. Indeed, such a bisexuality cannot be identified, because the tabooed subject is internalised as a prohibiting agent and, therefore, there are no foundational desires.

However, if Butler were to postulate a 'true' foundational sexuality, then it would not be *bi*sexual at all: that is to say it would not be made up of two types of drive or desire focusing on two objects, rather it would be one type of desire that does not discriminate amongst its objects. In other words, it would treat each 'object' as though it were undifferentiated. But this leads us back to Freud's 'polymorphously perverse' drives. These are genuinely undifferentiated: both as far as the nature of the drive is concerned, and as regards the type of object.

At this stage in the development of sexuality, Butler might argue, though, there is nothing for the ego to work on to contribute to the formation of gender identity. However, I disagree with Butler on several further counts. Butler reads 'castration' metaphorically as the fear of 'feminisation' associated within heterosexual culture with homosexuality. However, it is difficult to see how this 'fear' could be a real one for the boy. The 'threat of castration' in the commonplace sense can plausibly be identified as real for the boy, as Freud argues, because of the loss of other things he has valued – the breast (for some boys), his faeces, his favourite toy, for example. But it is difficult to see how Butler's metaphorical 'fear of feminisation' could be a real one for the boy. If she reads this threat, as she no doubt would, as purely an unconscious one that operates at the level of internalisation of taboos, then it is difficult to see why it should occur at the Oedipal stage. The internalising of cultural taboos continues and changes throughout one's life, and there are no clear external reasons why the Oedipal stage should play a primary role. Indeed, to suggest that the internalisations operate purely at the unconscious level, at this stage, in this way, is to make Freud's theory true-by-definition: there is no evidence that could confirm it.

I have a further difficulty with Butler's reading of Freud. This has to do with her association of 'feminisation' with homosexuality. Many little boys exhibit very strong feelings towards one another – love for one another and partial identification with one another (as well as in fantasy, identification with all sorts of other figures) – whilst demonstrating a wholesale rejection of 'feminisation'. On Butler's reading of Freud, this might demonstrate a rejection of the 'homosexual disposition' alongside a retention of the homosexual love object. But is it not implausible to hypostatise an internalisation of the taboo against the homosexuality disposition (the internalisation of the 'prohibition') alongside a retention of the same sex love object? What could it possibly mean? What sense would it make? Why would it be taboo? Is not a more likely explanation the following: gender identity has a multiplicity of possible causes, some of which may be genetic, others social and cultural, and it is possible to separate out some of these causes from heterosexual or homosexual *desires*.

The commonplace reading of Freud has a certain plausibility if certain assumptions (taken for granted in nineteenth century Vienna) are made: that children are largely brought up, in their early years, by female carers and that these carers are perceived as 'prohibiting' agents. Without these assumptions, of course, it is a lot less plausible. Yet, Butler's reading, surely, is less plausible still, in that a further assumption has to be built in: that the child is, in some way, aware of cultural taboos. Certainly there are taboos, on hitting people for example, of which children become aware very early on, but Butler's generalisation from this seems unlikely to be true.

To conclude the discussion so far, I would argue that Butler has not shown that 'the illusion of sexuality before the law is a creation of the law', because she has not offered a reading of Freud which makes sense of the development of sexuality and gender in children. I shall have more to say, in a more positive vein, on these issues in later chapters.

I would like now to move on to look at another kind of postmodern writing, and another kind of postmodern feminist scepticism: namely scepticism about 'universalising' and 'essentialist' feminisms.

Social Criticism without Philosophy

In what has become one of the classical statements on the subject, their article 'Social Criticism without Philosophy', Nancy Fraser and Linda Nicholson seek to lay the groundwork for a possible 'postmodern feminism'.[10] Initially, they point out, their 'encounter' between the two 'political–cultural currents' will be a trading of criticisms. However, their hope and expectation is that matters will not rest there.

They sketch out some conditions they believe are required for a post-modern feminism. They claim that such a feminism need not forswear all theory. Theory, however, must be 'explicitly historical' and 'non-universalist'. It would also 'dispense with the subject of history'. They are critical of a number of earlier feminists' theories on the ground that these theories are 'essentialist and monocausal'. They further describe the work of these feminists, in Lyotardian vein, as 'quasi metanarratives'. Theories of this type are 'large, social theories' 'which claim, for example, to identify causes and constitutive features of sexism that operate cross-culturally' (p. 27). They argue that the theories 'assume methods and concepts which are uninflected by temporality or historicity and which therefore function *de facto* as permanent, neutral matrices for inquiry' (p. 27). Such views, they argue, falsely universalise features of the theo-rist's own 'era, society, culture, class, sexual orientation and ethnic or racial group'.

This viewpoint is becoming commonplace in much feminist writing. The exposure by writers like bell hooks, Gloria Joseph, Audré Lord, and Elizabeth Spelman in the US, and Prathibha Parma, Nira Yuval-Davies and others in the UK of the implicit reference to white women in many feminist texts, and the pinpointing of heterosexist bias by, e.g., Adrienne Rich, has made many feminists doubt the possibility of making universal claims about women or of providing a universal theory of women's oppression.

One writer has put it thus: 'there are no common areas of experience between the wife of a plantation owner in the pre-Civil War South and the female slaves her husband owns'. This writer argues that gender is so thoroughly fragmented by race, class, historical particularity and indi-vidual difference, as to self-destruct as an analytical category. The 'bonds of womanhood', she insists, 'is a feminist fantasy borne out of the ethno-centrism of white, middle class academics'.[11]

It is important to point out, however, that early 'generalising' feminists were responding, in a fashion that is redolent of some postmodernist claims, to humanisms that purported to speak on behalf of 'humanity' without distinction of class or race. These feminists argued that such claims were specious, and disguised the fact that they were normally universalising from the experience of men. 'Universalising' feminisms, in other words, are postmodernist to the extent that they point to the often limited and partial character of the concept 'humanity'. Thus Mary Wollstonecraft was 'deconstructing' the humanist subject in her demand for women to be offered 'rights' like men.

There are, moreover, problems with the Lyotardian critique of 'grand narratives'.

Lyotard

In *The Postmodern Condition*,[12] Lyotard argues that knowledges, in contemporary post-Second World War societies – the 'postindustrial' age – tend not to be legitimated by their truth, but by their utility. 'The question now asked by the professional student, the state or institutions of higher education is no longer "Is it true?" but "What use is it?".' 'The value of knowledge', he suggests, 'is increasingly becoming instrumental'. (p. 51).

In particular, he claims that:

> The relationship of the suppliers and users of knowledge to the knowledge they supply and use is now tending, and will increasingly tend, to assume the form already taken by the relationship of commodity producers and consumers to the commodities they produce and consume. ... Knowledge is and will be produced in order to be sold. (p. 4)

Knowledge, he argues, has become the principal force of production. In this context of the mercantilisation of knowledge, more often than not the question 'Is it true?' is equivalent to 'Is it saleable?' (p. 51). In contemporary society, Lyotard suggests, 'knowledge and power are simply two sides of the same question' (pp. 8–9).

Lyotard argues that science is now legitimated by its 'performativity'. The truth criterion, in other words, is superseded by that of efficiency in performance: knowledge has become a commodity that must obey the market. Science, in contemporary societies, is concerned with 'fracture, catastrophes, paradox, the unintelligible'. It advances by searching for and 'inventing' counterexamples; supporting an argument means searching for a 'paradox' and legitimating it with new rules in the game of reasoning. Lyotard relies extensively for these claims on approaches to philosophy of science developed by theorists like Thomas Kuhn and Paul Feyerabend.

Lyotard believes that, in the context of the technological transformation now taking place, recourse to a 'grand narrative' or a totalising theory is no longer appropriate. The 'grand narrative' purported to be a universal metanarrative, grounding the truth of other narratives. He argues that such grand narratives are no longer credible. He encapsulated 'postmodernism' itself in the phrase 'incredulity towards metanarratives'.

The three specific features to which Lyotard objects in 'grand narratives' like the Enlightenment picture of the relentless progress of reason and freedom, Hegel's dialectic of spirit and Marx's materialist account of history are these. First, he dislikes their overarching character; second, he has reservations about their *foundationalism* – their desire to place knowledge on claims that are known with certainty; and third, he is sceptical about their optimistic faith in *progress*. Since grand 'metanarratives' which purport to guarantee which stories are right or true are no longer tenable, the idea that there is progress in history can no longer be upheld. Progress, he suggests, has become unintelligible on account of the paralogical invention that dominates the 'language game' of science. (By this, Lyotard means activity that is somehow beyond reason.) The 'Enlightenment' project, Lyotard argues, has foundered on the rock of the tragedy of Auschwitz. Foundationalism, according to Lyotard, no longer holds water. Any so-called metadiscourse is, in fact, just one more 'discourse' amongst others. In postmodern societies, the metanarrative of legitimation 'is being dispersed in clouds of narrative language elements' (p. xxiv).

Lyotard's picture of the nature of contemporary science has not, however, gone unquestioned. As Richard Rorty has put it: 'To say that "science aims" at piling paralogy on paralogy is like saying that "politics aims" at piling revolution on revolution. No inspection of the concerns of contemporary science . . . could show anything of the sort'.[13] There are individuals in contemporary science who are still looking for unifying theories.[14] Furthermore, Lyotard argues that critiques of empiricist philosophy of science, such as that of Kuhn, are indicative of a change in the practice of science, but they are not indicative of this at all; rather they are critiques of theoretical approaches to science that are seen to be misguided.[15] The theoretical approach of Feyerabend and Kuhn, therefore, does not entail or lead to the Lyotardian picture of the practice of science.

Lyotard argues that we must abandon the notion of progress because 'unintelligible' paralogical invention dominates scientific activity. Scientific practice has become a game of playing off incommensurable theories against one another. I think that this notion of incommensurability requires explanation that Lyotard does not himself provide. I should like, therefore, to examine the thesis as it appears in the work of Paul Feyerabend. Feyerabend provides a clear account of what incommensurability means. I believe not only that the Feyerabendian theoretical approach does not indicate a transformation in the practice of science, but that there are limitations in the theoretical approach itself.

Feyerabend on Incommensurability

In his writings, Feyerabend emphasises a discontinuity from one scientific theory to another at the level of their respective *methods*. He questions the distinction between method in the sense of rules employed in the discovery of theories and principles of evaluating rival theories. Referring to either of these senses of method, he says: 'The idea of a method that contains firm, unchanging and absolutely binding principles for conducting the business of science meets considerable difficulty when confronted with the results of historical research.'[16]

Feyerabend argues that methods alter as scientific theories change. One cannot compare theories by reference to a single method, because the latter alters with the former. For the variation of method, however, to have incommensurability in the radical sense that Lyotard appears to have in mind, as a consequence, namely that no two theories can be compared with one another, one would have to hold that *every* methodological principle altered from theory to theory. If it were just some principles that differed, for instance, in Einstein's theory and Newton's, so long as these were not principles determining the meanings of terms, the two theories could be compared. The theories could be compared by employing the methodological principles which were held in common by the two theories. Indeed, even if the two theories did differ totally in method, it would still be possible to compare them. They could be compared by employing one set of methodological principles, giving a justification of them and imposing them (of course inaccurately in fact) on the other theory. So even on the thesis of complete methodological variation – which could be Feyerabend and Lyotard's position – it is in principle possible to compare scientific theories. It is possible, on this view of incommensurability, therefore, to say that Newton's theory is incompatible with that of Einstein and that Einstein represents a development over Newton. If this, therefore, is Lyotard's view of incommensurability, it does not have the consequences for scientific practice to which he alludes.

What about variation in presuppositions? One could employ parallel arguments here against this variation tending to lead to radical incommensurability between theories. Again, this sense of incommensurability would not lead to Lyotard's view of the practice of science.

On these two senses of incommensurability, therefore, it is possible, *contra* Lyotard, to compare and contrast scientific theories. Neither of the two types of alteration from theory to theory described so far leads to incommensurability in the radically unacceptable sense. Feyerabend, however, also holds another type of incommensurability. He believes that the meaning of each term in a theory is determined by its role within the theory. Meaning determines reference. (And this applies in the case of all terms: there is no distinction between 'observational' and 'theoretical' terms.) So one and the same term in two theories will differ in sense and will pick out different objects. He says:

> extending the concepts of a new theory, T, to all its consequences, observational reports included, may change the interpretation of these consequences to such an extent that they disappear from the consequence classes either of earlier theories or of the available alternatives. These earlier theories and alternatives will then become incommensurable with T. The relation between special relativity (SR) and classical mechanics (CM) is a case in point.

The concept of length as used in SR and the concept of length presupposed in CM are different concepts. Both are *relational* concepts, and very complex relational concepts at that. . . . But relativistic length, or relativistic shape, involves an element that is absent from the classical concept and is in principle excluded from it. It involves the relative velocity of the object concerned in some reference system.[17] (Feyerabend's italics)

On this interpretation of incommensurability, no two theories can be compared, because the corresponding concepts differ in meaning.

On this view of Feyerabend's, the meaning of a term determines its reference. It follows, therefore, that Newton was not referring to anything by his use of the term 'mass' because we won't find anything with the properties he associates with mass. Therefore all Newton's assertions using the term 'mass' were false. Newton's theory, on these Feyerabendian assumptions, becomes completely false.

However, this interpretation of meaning can be questioned. Feyerabend says, of relativistic mass, that the concept is a relation, involving relational velocities; whereas Newtonian mass is a property of an object and is independent of the behaviour of the coordinate system. He says further:

The attempt to identify the classical mass with the relativistic rest mass is of no avail either. For although both may have the same numerical value, the one is still dependent on the coordinate system chosen (in which it is at rest and has that specific value) whereas the other is not so dependent.[18]

Now we may agree with Feyerabend that the Newtonian can identify the mass of a body without understanding it as related to a given coordinate or inertial system, whereas the Einsteinian cannot do this. However, this is not at all the same thing as admitting that the Einsteinian and the Newtonian can never refer to the same thing. This would only follow on certain assumptions about meaning. Only if we suppose that we need to know all of the properties that are held true of a thing, in order to refer to it, are we led to the conclusion that Newton and Einstein do not pick out the same thing. We can, however, allow that the two identify the same thing – mass – so long as each holds some of the properties to be true of mass that the other does. And, broadly, Newton and Einstein could be said to agree on the procedures for measuring mass. Only on very particular assumptions about meaning, therefore, does the 'irrational' view of science held by Lyotard hold. I shall have more to say about meaning in Chapter 3.

Therefore, on two possible senses of the notion of 'incommensurability' the irrational consequences about scientific practice that Lyotard describes do not follow. The third sense of it, moreover, relies on a questionable view of meaning. One of the main arguments for Lyotard's view that science is just one 'narrative' amongst others therefore is questionable. He has not demonstrated that science is not a distinctive practice governed by a commitment to progress and truth.

Back to Fraser and Nicholson

Nicholson and Fraser recognise that Lyotard's theory has its limitations. They point out that there is an unclarity in his view that we do not need overarching theories. Lyotard argues, for example, that we cannot have a single overarching theory of justice. But, Nicholson and Fraser say, this claim is ambiguous. On the one hand, it might mean that normative visions are decentred and plural; on the other, it could mean that the larger project of legitimating a vision like that or any invitation to advocate multiple normative visions, presupposes, for its justification, reference to the overarching norms Lyotard appears to want to rule out.

They accept, therefore, that Lyotard's view is 'neither entirely self-consistent nor entirely persuasive'. Despite their reservations about his theory, however, they believe that 'totalising' feminisms have much to learn from him. Accepting, for the purposes of argument, Lyotard's critique of 'grand narratives', let us compare it with Fraser's and Nicholson's of 'totalising' feminist theories. The first point to note is that none of the latter are strictly *meta*theories in the same sense as, for example, Marx's theory of history. One of the things Marx's theory of history does is offer an explanation of historical development – the movement from one mode of production to another – by hypostatising class struggle as the mechanism. Some Marxists – Althusser and Engels for example – would argue that he further postulates a metatheory – dialectical materialism – which seeks to found or guarantee the truth of the former. Totalising feminisms, however, are different. These kinds of feminism do neither of these things. Rather, they seek to explain an apparently obviously existent phenomenon – the oppression of women by men – by reference to some other notion: women's biology, their psychology, the universal structure of the family. The only analogous notion in Marx's theory is the explanation of class exploitation by economic factors. But, strictly speaking, this is not analogous, since class is defined, by Marx, by reference to one's relationship to the means of production. So, even if the latter is also explanatory of the former, it is also part of its definition, and hence crucially different from totalising feminist theories. Totalising feminisms are not metatheories in this sense then. But neither are they metatheories in another sense. They do not seek, as for example Marx does with his theory purporting to reveal the scientificity of historical materialism, to guarantee or to found the truth of the explanatory mechanism they postulate. There is no supraordinate theory in universalising radical feminisms, or socialist feminisms, that seeks to guarantee that explanatory appeals to biology or the family are correct. In this respect, then, these theories are not 'grand narratives' in Lyotard's sense: they are not 'foundationalist' theories.

Further, 'totalising' feminisms do not postulate a mechanism explaining historical progression as Marx does with the notion of class struggle, or Hegel with his dialectic of spirit. Rather, feminists of this kind seek a general and fundamental explanation of the oppression of women. Of course, they also hypothesise how things would be if this condition were removed, but this is different from postulating a mechanism explaining 'historical' progression.

Nicholson and Fraser do accept that the feminist theories are not strictly metanarratives in Lyotard's sense. They are not, they accept, 'historical normative theories about the trans-cultural nature of rationality or justice'. Rather, they are 'very large (empirical) social theories'. But, they argue, the theories in question are actually 'quasi meta narratives' – 'they tacitly presume some commonly held but unwarranted and essentialist assumptions about the nature of human beings' and 'methods and concepts which are uninflected by temporality or historicity'. Such theories, they argue, 'share some of the essentialist and ahistorical features of metanarratives' ('Social Criticism without Philosophy', p. 27).

This claim, of course, is a much weaker one than the full-blown attribution of 'metanarrative' status to the supposedly wrong-headed feminist theories. It is also a very different kind of claim. For it would be perfectly possible to believe in the metanarratives in the foundational sense, whilst upholding non-universalist, non-essentialist empirical theories. Indeed, some theorists who have upheld foundationalist metanarratives have allowed a wide variety in range of empirical theories. The verificationists, for instance, who propound a foundational metanarrative to the effect that all and only those theories that are empirically verifiable count as genuinely scientific, allow universal or particular, essentialist or non-essentialist empirical theories. The particular empirical 'theory' 'these swans are white' (said of two swans) is as legitimate as the universal theory 'all swans are white' on verificationist premises. One could indeed take almost any foundationalist metascientific theory of this type: Popperianism, Lakatos' viewpoint, realism – and the point would hold. The theory makes no particular claim about the universality or the essentialism of the empirical theories it purports to ground. So, the connection between Lyotardian metanarratives and the types of feminism of which Nicholson and Fraser are critical is tenuous. Many feminists might accept this point, however, and yet go along with Nicholson and Fraser's further point that theories of women's oppression that seek to identify universal, cross-cultural features of sexism are ahistorical.

It is not obvious, however, that employing the general concept 'woman' precludes recognition of historical and cultural diversity. Margaret Whitford[19] offers a helpful metaphor on this subject: feminist membership, she suggests, is like Merleau-Ponty's heap of sand, each grain individually is minute but·the total sandbank may block a river. Each grain, one might add, is different, but sufficiently alike to form the heap. Each woman is both different from every other and like every other. The philosopher of language Hilary Putnam's early work on 'natural kind' terms, 'gold', 'lead', may be illuminating here.[20] According to him, the sense of these words is fixed by their reference, and this is determined partly by their inner structures, and partly by 'the linguistic division of labour' through which the community of scientists acquired knowledge of their structure. Use of the natural kind term 'gold' does not lead to the belief that all that is gold is one type of gold. But, more importantly, use of the natural kind term is necessary in order to pinpoint the similarities in structure between gold watches, gold pens and gold coins. Similarly, use of the general term 'woman' may be necessary in order to pinpoint the commonalities between African peasant women, US white academic women and other women. The problem, of course, is that it is difficult, possibly unlike the case of gold, to describe what the 'essence' of women is. Yet diversity is only recognisable on condition that the concept 'woman' is identified. (This does not mean that the domain of its application is given with absolute precision, any more than one can do this with the natural kind term 'gold'.) Indeed, unless one does identify the category of woman (and other such categories) it is difficult to see how one can avoid a return to the particularism and individualism against which feminism originally set its face. If there is nothing but individuals, with no common characteristics, then one cannot speak of structural social features, such as discrimination against individuals as participants in social groupings. Correspondingly, the idea of a political community of women based on these shared characteristics, breaks down. *De dicto* essentialism in relation to the concept 'woman', therefore – the attempt to provide a general account or definition of 'women' – may be politically and linguistically necessary. These claims will be developed and expanded later on in the book.

Essentialism

This discussion has brought me to another claim made by Fraser and Nicholson about 'totalising' feminisms: their purported essentialism. Totalising feminisms, they suggest, 'share some of the essentialist and ahistorical features of metanarratives'.[21] Now the term 'essentialism' until recently took on the status of a term of abuse. To be guilty, according to some, of 'essentialism' was to commit a cardinal sin.

The term 'essentialism', like others of its ilk, was used to criticise theories as diverse as Marx's theory of history and feminisms ranging from Shulamith Firestone's theory to Kristeva and Irigaray's views. 'Essentialist' feminism, according to Lynne Segal for one, downplayed 'collective' political struggle in favour of an alternative emphasis on clearing our heads of 'male ideas' and 'male values'. Segal contrasted the essentialist project of much (eighties) feminism, 'which stresses basic differences between women and men, and asserts the moral and spiritual superiority of female experiences, values, characteristics and culture' with (an earlier socialist feminism) 'which stresses the social and economic disadvantages of women'.[22] For her, then, socialist-feminist theories escaped the mantle of essentialism. Fraser and Nicholson, however, would include some generalising socialist-feminist theories, which seek to minimise the importance of 'women's values' amongst essentialist theories.

What are the features of 'essentialism' that are generally thought to be objectionable? In a useful recent article, Jane Martin criticises the disabling use of the expression 'essentialism' as a form of condemnation.[23] She identifies several quite disparate readings for the expression in recent feminist literature. There is, first of all, the view that accidental properties of women – perhaps their purported 'peaceable natures' – are mistaken for essential ones; second, there is the attribution of a set of qualities that may be applicable only to some women, to all, and third, there is the claim that 'essentialism' is a form of 'biological reductionism'. The first two of these are acceptable as criticisms of a theory although, Martin argues, it is quite another matter to consign a view to the dustbin for upholding mistaken notions. The third, however, is not an acceptable criticism: essence talk is not necessarily about biology nor is biological talk necessarily about essences.

Firestone

I should like to have a look at the work of some of the thinkers who are accused by Fraser and Nicholson of 'essentialism' to see whether they can legitimately be described as essentialist in any of these senses. One such thinker is Shulamith Firestone. Her theory is perhaps the best known and the most forceful biological explanation of women's oppression. She extended Marx and Engels' materialist conception of history to the realm of the sexual. 'Beneath the economic' according to her, 'reality is psychosexual'.[24] There are, she says two basic classes, men and women, and the origin of this class division lies in biology. 'Sex class sprang from a biological reality; men and women were created different and not equal.'[25] 'Before the advent of birth control, women were at the continual mercy of their biology, menstruation, menopause and "female ills", constant painful childbirth, wet nursing and care of infants.'[26]

Firestone extends Marx and Engels' analysis by altering their wording. Here is her version of part of Engels' *Socialism, Utopian and Scientific*:

> Historical materialism is that view of the course of history which seeks the ultimate cause and the great moving power of all historical events in the (economic development of society) *dialectic of sex*: the division of society into *biological* classes for the purposes of *procreative* production and the struggle of these classes with one another: in the changes in the modes of (production and exchange) *marriage, reproduction and child care created by these struggles*.[27] (The italicised words are Firestone's insertions; Engels' original text appears in brackets.)

Instead of the economic, Firestone argues, the sexual–reproductive area of society furnishes the real basis upon which the superstructure of economic, juridical and political institutions arises.

What then, is to be done? If women's subordination is biologically determined, the consistent answer would appear to be: change female biology. Firestone agrees. Just as for Marx a condition of socialism is working class control of the means of production, so for her a condition of a 'classless' society is women controlling their means of reproduction. And this means ceasing to *bear* as well as rear children, for 'pregnancy is barbaric! it is the temporary deformation of the body of the individual for the sake of the species.'[28] It is proposed instead that test tube babies (made possible by developments in embryology and cybernetics) will facilitate a 'qualitative change in humanity's basic relation to both production and reproduction'.[29] These new relations will make possible the destruction of the class system and the family.

One difficulty with this is that it is difficult to transform a theory intended for one purpose to another context. According to the materialist conception of history, the economic base of society determines the nature of juridical and political institutions. Further, changes in modes of production are explained in terms of class struggle and by means of the conflict between the developing forces of production and the relations. Crudely, feudalism disappeared because its social relations came to act as fetters on the progression of the forces. Capitalism is to be replaced by socialism, according to the theory, when, with a sufficiently developed technology, the working class becomes conscious of *its* interests.

Firestone argues that 'sexual reproductive' reality conditions the economic, the ideological and other social phenomena. What could correspond to the forces and relations of production within 'sexual–reproductive' reality? What would count as a mode of production? And what would correlate with the class struggle? Perhaps the forces of production are replaced by the sexual organs – the 'tools'. And perhaps for 'modes of production' we should substitute families? Then, we should say, as the sexual organs change and develop so they come into conflict with the relations of reproduction. Maybe the male organ grew much larger with early changes in family form, and larger still with the institution of monogamy. But all this is approaching the realm of fantasy.

It is problematic, indeed, to describe women as a class. What do women as a group produce that constitutes the surplus, to be appropriated by men as a group? There is no one thing. It is questionable, indeed, as we have seen, whether one can talk of a common women's oppression, let alone whether it makes sense to speak of women as a class.

In the system Marx described as capitalism, it is in the interests of the ruling class to extract as much surplus value from the workers as possible, and one way to do this is by keeping wages low. The interests of the working class are necessarily the opposite. If we interpose Firestone's theory, however, it is only in partnerships where the one party gets satisfaction by ensuring that the other gets none, that the interests of the sexes are necessarily opposed.

There are problems with Firestone's theory, therefore. But is it 'essentialist' in any of Martin's senses? Firestone does not mistake accidental properties of women for essential ones, for she deliberately characterises women as a class on the basis of features which are shared by all women. For the same reason, she does not attribute qualities that may be true only of some women to all. Firestone's theory is certainly a theory that makes much of the biological domain, but it is not reductionist – it does not set out to reduce all qualities of women to the biological. To claim, furthermore, of Firestone, who deliberately applied Marx's materialist conception of history to the realm of the sexual, that it is ahistorical is a very odd claim to make.

The Domestic Labour Debate Theorists

Similar points could be made about another group of theorists who are described as 'essentialist' and 'ahistoricist' by Fraser and Nicholson – the protagonists of the domestic labour debate, as it came to be known.

In the seventies, socialist-feminists attempted to provide a theory linking the Marxist analysis of class with an account of the causes of women's oppression. A significant early version of such an 'integrated theory' was known as the 'domestic labour debate'. All discussants assumed a basic Marxist explanation of class exploitation. And, from Wally Seccombe's and Jean Gardiner's work onwards, contributions mushroomed.[30] All assumed that the family is the site of women's oppression. All argued further that the social and economic context of capitalist society (the predominant form taken by the mode of production throughout the world today) is significant in structuring the family. The form that male dominance takes on was thought therefore to be in some way dependent on historical period and social structure.

This domestic labour debate brought to light the significance of women's household work. Earlier feminists, for example Betty Friedan, had written about the stifling and stultifying nature of housework, particularly to middle class American women in the 1950s.[31] But it was not until the domestic labour debate began that the importance of domestic labour in the capitalist mode of production came to be adroitly addressed. In the course of the debate, questions like 'Does domestic labour produce value?' and 'Is it subject to the law of value?' were raised, and various answers offered. Some argued, for instance, that women houseworkers do not simply produce use-values; but, through activities like cooking, they are also creating labour-power. In other words, women houseworkers undertake work that contributes to the production of surplus value (see Seccombe and Gardiner). Critics of this view were quick to point out that the housewife as housewife does not sell her labour-power as commodity to her husband. There is nothing in the relationship between husband and wife comparable to a labour-contract. The housewife is not paid a wage.[32] The issue remains unresolved.

The terms of the domestic labour debate have indeed come in for criticism. The major criticisms feminists made of it were twofold: most of the early contributors to the discussion had argued that 'the family' exists because of the functions it fulfils in the capitalist mode of production, these functions supposedly explaining its origin. Critics claimed, however, that although the relationship between privatised domestic labour and the capitalist mode of production was outlined, and sometimes described in detail, the question *why* capitalist relations developed in such a way as to ensure women's subordination was never answered.[33] Additionally, a central and fundamental reservation critics had about the debate is that its contributors failed to explain why *women* do domestic labour and as a consequence, the domestic labour debate provided no solution at all to the original problem: what causes women's oppression? Finally, one could argue that the domestic labour debate fails to explain women's oppression (assuming for the moment, for the purposes of the argument, that there is such a thing) outside capitalism.

Again, therefore, there were problems with these theorists. But they were not essentialist in any of the misguided senses: they did not set out to describe a set of features that were shared by *all* women, so they neither mistook accidental properties of women for essential ones, nor did they attribute qualities that may be true of only some women, to all. Rather, they were deliberately describing the role of domestic labour within capitalist societies. Maybe they generalised too much within capitalism, but this does not make them essentialist theorists.

Chodorow

Similar points can, I believe, be made about another thinker chastised by Fraser and Nicholson as 'essentialist', Nancy Chodorow. Chodorow's theory struck a chord with many feminists in the late 1970s and 1980s.[34] She set out to give an account of the process which leads women to reproduce their inferiority. She postulated a universal activity – mothering – to explain this phenomenon. Female mothering, she argued, produces and reproduces women whose deep sense of self is relational and men whose deep sense of self is not. Nicholson and Fraser share the sympathies of many feminists for this theory and yet they have reservations about the hypostatising of a single activity – mothering – which constitutes enough of an 'individual kind' to warrant one label. They reiterate their objections to the 'essentialism' of this model, but they add the further point that Chodorow's notion of a female 'relational' self and a male 'non-relational sense of self' becomes problematic when given any particular content. It cannot be spelled out as implying 'every human interaction' since men have typically been more concerned than women with some interactions 'e.g. those concerning the aggrandisement of power and wealth'. If, instead, it is spelled out as having to do with women's greater association with 'intimacy, love and friendship' then, Nicholson and Fraser argue, Chodorow is illegitimately generalising from features of modern western private life to all societies. The overriding point they make about theories like Chodorow's and other generalising theories like Catherine Mackinnon's, Ann Ferguson's and others, is that the general categories each presuppose 'group together activities that are not necessarily conjoined in all societies' ('Social Criticism without Philosophy', p. 31). They conclude, therefore, that any legitimate feminist theory must be 'explicitly historical, attuned to the cultural specificity of different societies and periods and that of different groups within societies and periods' (p. 34).

Chodorow's theory does seem to me to presuppose the phenomenon it sets out to explain – women's oppression. It assumes that women's mothering role already contains key features of this oppression which tend to be reproduced in little girls. However, there are, surely, sufficient common features of mothering for there to be one concept, playing a relatively uniform causal role in the way that Chodorow suggests. The key feature surely concerns the dual characteristics of identifying the child as belonging to the person in some sense, and playing a major role in caring for it. The features will be present to varying degrees in different family forms – in some cases the 'major' role being severely attenuated. Other aspects of the role are currently varying. This, correlatively, could be differentially reproduced. It may be that, unlike Firestone and the domestic labour debate theorists, Chodorow is essentialist in two of Martin's senses: she does appear to characterise what may be an accidental property of women – their mothering role – as in some way essential. Also, she does appear (mistakenly) to attribute this quality to all women. Yet, it seems to me that this is not sufficient as a criticism of the theory. The mothering role is one that substantial numbers of women have taken on, and unless we rule out such generalisations a priori, it remains an open question whether the role of women as mothers explains other aspects of their position and experience.

I do not accept, therefore, either that the label 'essentialist' allows us to dismiss 1970s and 1980s feminists' theories or that it is impossible to defend an 'essence' of woman. In a later chapter, I will advocate returning to a revamped biological view of this essence.

Concluding Remarks

Fraser and Nicholson, amongst recent feminists, as we have seen earlier, chastise feminist theory for its 'essentialism' and its 'ahistoricism'. In the 1970s the opposite term 'historicism' was often used, following the work of Louis Althusser, in a similarly negative way, to castigate a particular type of Marxism. Althusser, in *Reading Capital*, informs us that there are three ways of characterising the scientificity of political economy which turn out to be historicist ways of so doing. The three ways are:

1. the science 'reduces the phenomenon to the essence'[35]
2. the science 'is a systematic theory which embraces the totality of its object and seizes the "internal connection" which links together the "reduced" essences of *all* economic phenomena' (Althusser's italics)[36] and
3. the scientific theory 'historicises' the categories with which it deals. It treats as subject to change and development surplus value, rent and profit.

In other words, one of the arguments offered by Althusser against historicism – namely that it 'reduces the phenomenon to the essence' – is also proffered by some recent feminists as an argument against ahistoricism! Moreover, Althusser's reason for being critical of that reduction – that it presupposes a continuity of object between the various stages of a science, is again very similar to the postmodernist feminist critique of earlier 'universalising' feminists – that they presuppose a continuity, over time, in the nature of women.

As if this was not enough, there are similarities, indeed, between Althusser's critique of 'empiricism' (another expression he used in a critical sense) and recent feminists' objections to essentialism. Althusser argued that the empiricist believed (mistakenly) that 'to know is to abstract from the real object its essence, the possession of which by the subject is then called knowledge.' Postmodernist feminists, as we have seen, have criticised 'essentialism' for the same sorts of reason.

This discussion should lead us to treat with caution Fraser and Nicholson's claim that a postmodern feminism should be explicitly historical and non-universalist. I have not, of course, shown that it should not be these things, but I have, I hope, sown some seeds of doubt as to whether the earlier feminist theories that have recently tended to be rejected out of hand, can so easily be dismissed on the ground that they are *not* these things.

In this chapter, I have expounded the views of some theorists who are sceptical on the one hand about the category 'woman' and, on the other, about universalising and essentialist feminisms. I have expressed reservations about each of these types of scepticism. I should like to move on, in the next chapter, to look at another thinker whose work has been inspirational for recent postmodernist/poststructuralist feminism.

2

Irigaray, Lacan and Derrida

One feminist whose work is particularly significant in the terrain of post-modernism and feminism is Luce Irigaray. Like Butler, Irigaray stresses the way in which conceptualisations of 'woman' have been caught up in particular 'phallocentric' frameworks. Irigaray deploys the feminine to subvert 'phallogocentric' logic.

Until recently, ironically, Irigaray's work, alongside that of the thinkers mentioned in Chapter 1, was castigated as essentialist.[1] More recently, however, feminist writers in the UK and the USA have begun to argue that certain French writers, who focus on women's *difference* from men, are not essentialist thinkers. British and American feminists are beginning to see that, for the French writers, the nature of the difference between men and women has been 'one of the most controversial areas of debate'.[2] The work of these French writers is therefore now beginning to be seen as deserving of discussion, in the UK, in its own right.[3]

Indeed, many postmodern feminists see the creation of a female symbolic and feminine subjectivity to be *imperative* for feminism. According to this way of thinking, the mainstay of women's oppression lies in a symbolic system that is dominated, in Whitford's words, by the 'male imaginary'.[4] Correlatively, this system depends upon the identification of subjectivity with rationality and the exclusion of the female as 'other'. Influenced by, although critical of, psychoanalysis and poststructuralism, the inspirational writings of Irigaray are pivotal for such feminists. Irigaray is a centrally important feminist and philosopher of 'difference'. I should like, in the next few chapters, to trace some of the roots of Irigaray's thinking, and to articulate my disagreements with some of the ideas which are significant, both for her and for a number of postmodern feminists.

Two of Luce Irigaray's most widely read works, published in French in 1974 and 1977 respectively, are *Speculum of the Other Woman*[5] and *This Sex which is Not One*.[6] In these texts she sets out to do something different from theorising the nature of 'women'. 'I can answer neither *about* nor *for* women . . . it is no more a question of my making women the *subject* or the *object* of a theory than it is of subsuming the feminine under some general term, such as "women".'[7]

Like Butler, Irigaray would say that one cannot define 'woman', for so doing would be to conceptualise the relation between the sexes in terms of polarity and opposition, and this would be to remain caught in 'phallocentric', 'logocentric' discourse. (These terms will be explained later.) On the other hand, as Jane Gallop explains: 'Without a female homosexual economy, a female narcissistic ego, a woman in a heterosexual encounter will always be engulfed by the male homosexual economy, will not be able to represent her difference.'[8]

Women must, therefore, according to Irigaray, have available to them symbolisations of their 'otherness' which are not reducible to a simple definition of 'woman'. One cannot, she says, 'simply' keep to the outside of phallocentrism.[9]

Irigaray's thought owes a lot to two male French thinkers: Jacques Derrida and Jacques Lacan. Although, as Toril Moi said: 'Irigaray never acknowledges the fact, her analysis of male specular logic is deeply indebted to Derrida's critique of the western philosophical tradition.'[10] This word 'critique' is infected with the notion Derrida and Irigaray deconstruct; yet it is true that, like Derrida, Irigaray offers 'deconstructive' readings of figures in the history of western philosophy. Again, like Derrida, it is *philosophical* texts upon which Irigaray focuses. Philosophy, she says, is the 'discourse that we have to challenge in as much as this discourse sets forth the law on all discourses, in as much as it constitutes the discourse on discourses'.[11] And, despite the fact that Irigaray's publication of her doctoral thesis, *Speculum of the Other Woman*, led to her expulsion from Lacan's Ecole Freudienne at Vincennes, her work is strongly indebted to Lacan's writings. I should like to preface my discussion of Irigaray, in this chapter, by looking at some aspects of the work of these two theorists of 'postmodernity', in order to highlight some presuppositions that are significant both for Irigaray and for other postmodern feminists.

I will begin with Derrida, focusing on his 'analysis' of a text of Jean Jacques Rousseau, both because I believe this analysis is useful for understanding Derrida, and because it concerns an area of debate that closely resembles many of the discussions Irigaray takes up on femininity.

Derrida on the Speaking Subject

In his book *Of Grammatology* Jacques Derrida presented his reflections on 'being as presence' or 'logocentrism'. Derrida's 'science of writing' consists in these disquisitions. According to him, the 'logocentric tradition' (this for Derrida consists, as it turns out, of most of the western philosophical tradition) assumes a speaking subject, whose thoughts are clearly presented to it, and whose speech reflects its thoughts. Intuitively, given this characterisation of the notion of the subject, one would have thought that the clearest example of it would be the Cartesian self. For, in the case of Descartes' subject, the speech sound 'I think' represents the thought 'I think', and the subject – the thinking subject – is 'present' as the thought to speech. Derrida, however, does not take the Cartesian self as paradigmatic of this view. Instead, one central example of it, he thinks, appears in a work by Jean Jacques Rousseau: *Essay on the Origin of Languages*. It is Rousseau's notion of the subject, rather than Descartes', upon which Derrida chooses to direct some of his attention. Derrida says: 'For purposes of this identification [discursive articulation of the logocentric epoch] Rousseau seems to us to be the most revealing.'[12] The logocentric subject is revealed through a discussion of Rousseau's views on language.

As others have pointed out,[13] it is odd, on the surface, for Derrida to have decided to take Rousseau's *Essay* to be the focal point for his discussion of logocentrism, for at least two reasons.

One is that, even in the French philosophical tradition, the *Essay* is usually taken to be marginal in Rousseau's thought; and the other is that the view of language presented by Rousseau in the *Essay* is one which challenges the received Enlightenment/post-Enlightenment view on the subject. Rousseau doubts and questions the Enlightenment view of progress. Yet it is characteristic of Derrida to take apparently marginal texts as being as important as those normally regarded as being central in the presentation of an issue. Elsewhere he chastises J. L. Austin, for instance, for setting aside 'parasitic' uses of language in favour of a discussion of 'serious' discourse.[14] Doing this, Derrida makes out, begs the questions of the appropriateness of focusing mainly on non-parasitic uses of language.

But it is interesting, nonetheless, that Derrida should take as his 'target' Rousseau's *Essay*. The *Essay* argues that the vital role of language lies in the expression of feelings, cries and gestures and not, as many thinkers have argued, ideas. Additionally, Rousseau's view of the origin of language differs from that of many writers on the subject. Instead of claiming, as many have done, that language comes into being as a means for expressing needs, Rousseau argues that it is not needs but *passions* that give rise to the first vocal utterances: 'fruit does not appear from our hands: we can eat it without speaking; and one stalks in silence the prey on which one would feast. But for moving a young heart, or repelling an unjust aggressor, nature dictates tones of voice, cries, lamentations.'[15]

Rousseau's text is a logocentric one, for Derrida, in this sense: (a) individual units of meaning appear to be fully intelligible on their own, without recourse to any other concept; and (b) utterances seem to be meaningful directly and intuitively, without presupposing any system of utterances. One might say that a subject who feels pain or cries is self-present to itself in a way that a thinking subject is not. The subject who feels pain is one whose 'whole essence', one might say, is revealed in the pain. There is no doubting (at least so many have argued) the fact that when I am in pain, it is I who am in pain. The feeling of pain is prior to the expression of any thought at all. Thus, arguably, the subject is present to itself in its feelings in a more immediate way than is the thinking self. For the Cartesian self must already have developed the conception of a thought and a self before it can reveal itself through its thinking. One might support Derrida's view that Rousseau's *Essay* constitutes a better example of logocentrism, being-as-presence, than Descartes' *Meditations* in this way.

But there is a further reason why Derrida focuses on Rousseau in particular. This is that Rousseau's text 'deconstructs' itself. It can itself be taken as an example of 'Grammatologie'. It can be seen as exemplifying 'arché writing': that sort of writing that undermines the self-presence of speech. Arché writing demonstrates the play of language, the elusive substitution at work in it, that is common both to the old sense of writing and to speech. Indeed, Derrida would say the same sort of thing about almost any writer whose works he discusses.

In order to discuss Rousseau on the language of gesture, Derrida refers, additionally, to others of Rousseau's writings: *The Confessions, The Discourses* and *Emile*.

In these writings, Rousseau discusses the 'state of nature'. In the original state of nature, for Rousseau a hypothetical pre-social arrangement of human beings, there is no language, no separation between self and other. Needs are satisfied, but, so long as this is the case, no expressions are required to symbolise them. Yet, as some people begin to acquire property, and inequalities develop, emotions, like jealousy, begin to appear. And these emotions, Rousseau argues, require linguistic expression. At this point, a distinction between self and other begins to develop, and people begin to see themselves through the eyes of others.

Superficially, the early stage of Rousseau's thinking is not useful at all for Derrida's description of his work as logocentric. For if the self cannot distinguish itself from others, as appears to be the case in the early state of nature, then it has no sense of itself at all. But one might argue that, in a certain extended sense, the logocentric self *is* revealed in Rousseau's early state of nature. Rousseau describes the relationship between mother and child as the paradigmatically natural relationship. The child initially both identifies with and desires the mother. Hence love for another – an emotion – can be present before the child is able to distinguish itself from its mother. The emotion is present as a diffuse, generalisable 'love' which just so happens to focus on one person: the mother. Yet love for the mother is also self-love, for the child is not yet distinct from its mother. Therefore, in a certain sense, the logocentric subject is revealed here: the subject is present to itself through its love for its mother. This generalised love is both subject and object for the child: this child is itself a loving self that directs its love on itself (the mother).

This point is illustrated further. In *The Discourse on the Origin of Inequality* Rousseau argues that there are two hypothetical states of nature. After the acquisition of property, described earlier, Rousseau claims that ambition rises up and instils in people desires to harm one another. When all the land has been allocated, the only way anyone can get more is at another's expense. Riots ensue. A tyrant emerges, whose driving ambition is pure greed. The people revolt and, after the period of inequality, a new state of nature with a new-found equality emerges. This new state of nature, according to Rousseau, is peculiar to human beings, and in it the pre-eminent natural sentiment or virtue is 'pity'. Indeed, it is sometimes even present in the previous state of nature:

> I am speaking of compassion [pitié] which is a disposition suit-able to creatures so weak and subject to so many evils as we certainly are: by so much the more universal and useful to mankind, as it comes before any kind of reflection; and at the same time so natural, that the very brutes themselves sometimes give proofs of it.[16]

Pity, therefore, for Rousseau, is a pre-eminently natural feeling. Natural pity, indeed, 'is illustrated archetypically by the relation between mother and child'.[17] 'Natural pity commands like a gentle voice. In the metaphor of the soft voice, the presence of the mother as well as of Nature is at once brought in.'[18]

Thus, the logocentric subject is revealed in the way I have described: through the 'natural' sentiment of pity, focused, in a generalised way, by the child on the mother. This focusing is also, as I have argued, a directing on the self.

Yet one might say that Rousseau's text also 'deconstructs' itself. Pity, for him, is both supremely natural and precisely that which, by its very nature, renders culture necessary. Naturally, pity is universally directed. It is not focused specifically on one person. In fact, as we have seen, for the child, pity is focused exclusively on the mother, but the mother, for the child, serves to represent anyone to anyone. But pity, also, for Rousseau is that which brings about the undoing of the natural. Pity is both supremely natural, since, without it, there would be no relation between mother and child, and therefore no relations between humans at all. And yet, the specifically human expression of pity requires charac-teristics that take us out of nature and into culture. Rousseau argues that the *human* expression of pity requires the exercise of the imagination. The exercise of the imagination, he believes, distinguishes human beings from animals. The imagination, for Rousseau, in Derrida's words, 'broaches history'.[19]

Let me expand a little, to explain Rousseau's meaning here. In a way, ideally, for Rousseau, nature should be self-sufficient. A natural state is one where all needs are provided for; desires are satisfied. And yet, for Rousseau, although in a sense the state of nature is self-sufficient, it is also lacking. How is this? Let us take the mother/child symbiosis once more to explain this notion. As I have already said, this relationship is a paradigmatically natural one. The child suckles at the breast in order to survive; the mother enables it to survive. And yet nature is lacking in several ways. First of all, some babies may be deprived of mothers (as Rousseau himself was in fact). Another respect in which nature is lacking is that, were all the child's needs and desires to be satisfied, that would be too much for it – such a state would be, according to Rousseau, equivalent to death: 'If I had even in my life tasted the delights of love even once in their plenitude, I do not imagine that my frail existence would have been sufficient for them, I would be dead in the act.'[20] 'Pleasure itself, without symbol or supplement, would be only another name for death'.[21] Thus, were nature to allow itself free reign, that would be equivalent to annihilation. The full expression of natural emotions, for Rousseau, and pity is no exception here, leads to the annihilation of the self. But in their natural state, emotions *demand* full, generalisable expression. Thus, the natural expression of emotion is, in the end, impossible for humans, and emotions have to be expressed in other, culturally bound, ways. Rousseau's route to these culturally bound manifestations of emotion is via the imagination, which allows their symbolic expression in the absence of the actual object of the emotion.

Nature is lacking and the natural expression of emotion for humans is impossible, in further senses, for Rousseau. The mother, and nature, too, symbolised by the mother, cannot satisfy all the child's demands for she would be annihilated if she did. Thus the natural symbiosis is broken once again. And also nature is lacking in this sense: the child's love for the mother leads to self-love. When the mother fails to satisfy its demands, the child turns, as Freud was to argue, its love on itself, in the form of onanism (thumb sucking, etc.).

Onanism, however, necessarily leads away from nature, since it is intrinsically symbolic: it provides constant imaginary presences. Onanism works only by imagining constant others. It therefore depends upon the possibility of symbolisation, and it leads away from nature. Finally, human beings, by their very natures, their capacities to generalise, for instance, are led away from nature. Perfectibility requires that they are. Pity, that most natural of emotions, is an emotion directed on another. Yet, by that very token, it is not natural, since relating to another requires something that is not natural: the possibility of symbolisation. Natural pity, in fact, in the end, requires the imagination for its expression.

Rousseau's writings, then, provide an illustration of Derrida's notion and 'critique' of logocentrism. Logocentric texts, he claims, necessarily 'deconstruct' themselves. All philosophers in the western philosophical tradition are said to 'fall foul' of the notion. Derrida offers similar readings of other thinkers, showing how their thought is supposed to do so. Despite appearances to the contrary, philosophers whose views seem to be as diverse as Plato, Descartes and Husserl in fact are 'logocentric' thinkers.

By means of this reading of Rousseau's text we can illustrate the only alternative, according to Derrida, to logocentrism or 'being-as-presence', the view that

> there has never been anything but writing: there have never been anything but supplements, substitutive signifiers which could only come forth in a chain of differential references. . . . Nature, that which words like 'real mother' name, have already escaped, have never existed; that which opens meaning and language is writing as the disappearance of natural presence.[22]

Rousseau's pity illustrates Derrida's notion of the supplement. According to one version of Derrida's reading of Rousseau, writing supplements speech: it is added to it; it is not natural. Pity is a supplement to nature: it is an example of supplementarity in general in so far as it both adds to what it supplements (in this case, nature) and reveals an inherent lack in what it supplements. Rousseau also discusses education as a supplement to nature. Nature is in principle complete, a natural plenitude to which, as Culler puts it: 'education is an external addition'. But, Culler continues,

> the description of this supplementation reveals an inherent lack in nature; nature must be completed – supplemented – by education if it is to be truly itself: the right education is needed if human nature is to emerge as it truly is. The logic of the supplement thus makes nature the prior term, a plenitude that is there at the start, but reveals an inherent lack or absence within it, so that education, the additional extra, also becomes an essential condition of that which it supplements.[23]

In the end, as Culler argues, what Rousseau's supplements reveal is an endless chain of supplements. Writing is a supplement to speech. 'Languages are made to be spoken,' writes Rousseau. 'Writing serves only as a supplement to speech.'[24] The supplement is an inessential extra, added to something that is already complete; but it is also added in order to complete that something, to compensate for what is lacking in the original. But speech is itself already a supplement: 'children' says Emile, quickly learn to use speech 'to supplement their own weaknesses'.[25]

For Derrida, there is no such thing as reference in language, rather all terms are essentially incomplete. Each term is a supplement to every other.

I have used this reading of Derrida on Rousseau to illustrate a number of 'central' Derridean concepts: his view of writing, his 'critique' of the notion of 'being-as-presence' and logocentrism, and his idea of the 'supplement'. Irigaray draws on many of these notions.

Lacan

Irigaray's indebtedness to Lacan is more closely acknowledged in her writings than is her debt to Derrida. A chapter headed 'Cosi fan tutti' of *Le Sexe qui n'en est pas un* is devoted to him; her use of the term 'imaginary', which occurs throughout her writings, owes much to the Lacanian 'imaginary', and the term 'Speculum' itself is partly a critique of Lacan's concept of 'mirror'.

Like Freud, Lacan set out to explain how individuals become human. Both assume that people are not born human, rather they become so through incorporation in the cultural order. Lacan registers Freud's break with psychologies based on humanist categories: 'as a result of [Freud's] discovery the very nature of the human was no longer to be found at the place assigned to it by a whole humanist tradition.'[26]

He develops a critique of the Freudian theory of the Ego. Freud's first picture of the Ego has it representing the external world; the Ego controls the limitless demands of the individual's libido for satisfaction. The Ego is, therefore, a force that curtails primarily biological drives. Freud upholds this view as early as the time of writing of the largely determinist text: 'Project for a Scientific Psychology', published in 1895.[27] With the publication in 1914 of his paper 'On Narcissism', however, Freud alters his view somewhat to claim that the Ego can itself be the focus for libidinal drives; indeed that it is the primary locus of these drives.[28] Additionally, for Freud, personal identity comes to be seen as something that develops. 'A unity comparable to the ego cannot exist in the individual from the start; the ego has to be developed.'[29] Ego-libido (energy focused on the self) is transferred, in this process of change, onto object-libido. But as more libido is invested in the object, the more impoverished becomes the Ego. To counter this, the Ego chooses to model itself on itself. In 'The Ego and the Id', Freud argues that: 'the ego is first and foremost a bodily ego.'[30] Freud expands on this: 'the ego is ultimately derived from bodily sensations, chiefly from those springing from the surface of the body. It may thus be regarded as a mental projection of the surface of the body besides representing the superficies of the mental apparatus.' Freud continues to argue, however, that the Ego has special access to external reality.

This view of the Ego is explicitly rejected by Lacan. Self-identity, for him, is an alienating, imaginary process. In his 1936 essay 'The Mirror Stage as Formative of the Function of I as Revealed in Psychoanalytic Experience', Lacan reformulates some Hegelian concepts in his account of the formation of the Ego.[31] This rewriting of Hegel expresses the fundamental difference between the thought of Lacan on the subject and that of Freud. Lacan tends to reject the 'biologistic' aspects of Freud's thought, and to emphasise, rather, a reading of mental life much more akin to the hermeneutic notion of 'interpretative understanding'. He would argue, for example, that no biological event can have an unmediated effect on the formation of the subject, because the influence of this event depends on the way in which it is interpreted, and this in turn is conditioned by the intersubjective relations into which the subject enters.

Drawing on Hegel's master–slave dialectic in *The Phenomenology of Mind*,[32] Lacan argues that it is only through the recognition of the desire of the other that the self gains a sense of self.

Self-consciousness, according to Hegel, emerges out of the cycle of desire and its satisfaction. To crave an ice cream, one might say, is to experience oneself as lacking that ice cream. The satisfaction of the desire by the consumption of the ice cream reinforces the sense of self. Yet physical objects cannot perform this role in abiding fashion, for the satisfaction of the craving obliterates the 'lack' which gave rise to the sense of self. Only, Hegel argues, when desire is focused on another similarly placed subject, can the awareness of self properly emerge. Thus, the self gains a sense of self through the mediation of the other's desire.

Using this Hegelian dialectic, Lacan describes the beginnings of the formation of subjectivity on the part of the child. He invites us to imagine the child contemplating itself in a mirror. He describes how we see it begin to develop an integrated self-image. The child, who is still uncoordinated – he describes it as an 'hommelette', employing the ideas of the fluidity of an omelette, and of a 'little man' – finds reflected back onto itself in the mirror, a unified image of itself, a Gestalt. It arrives at a sense of itself as whole narcissistically, by means of an object outside it that is reflected back to it. Here is Lacan: 'We have only to understand the mirror stage as an *identification*, in the full sense that analysis gives to the term, namely the transformation that takes place in the subject when he assumes an image.'[33] The object is both part of ourselves – we identify with it – and alien to us. Lacan refers to paintings of Hieronymus Bosch to express the uncoordinated state of the child. In spite of its being merely a mass of limbs, it gains a sense of itself as whole and unified by means of its specular image. Again to quote Lacan: 'this jubilant assumption of his specular image by the child at the *infans* stage, still sunk in his motor incapacity and nursling independence, would seem to exhibit in an exemplary situation the symbolic matrix in which the I is precipitated in a primordial form.'[34] The mirror image is thus a misrecognition (méconnaissance) of the self – the child thinks of itself as whole and unified, but this sense of self is essentially an alienated, distorted one.

For Lacan, the gaining of a sense of self is inseparable ultimately from the acquisition of language. Outside 'discourse' there is no self, even an alienated, distorted self. 'Outside discourse', as many commentators have put it, 'is psychosis'.[35] The child acquires a sense of itself as whole and unified as it 'enters' language. Only when he or she can speak can the child properly become an agent in a social, cultural and symbolic environment.

In this context, the influence on Lacan is the structuralism of Saussure. This influence emerges most clearly in the 1955 *Discours de Rome*.[36] Saussure's claim that the relation between signifier and signified is an arbitrary one and that meaning is determined by the relations between signs profoundly affected Lacan.

Here he is: 'The first network, that of the signifier, is the synchronic structure of the language material in so far as in that structure each element assumes its precise function by being different from the others.' And 'the unity of signification proves never to be resolved into a pure indication of the real, but always refers back to another signification. That is to say, the signification is realised only on the basis of a grasp of things in their totality.'[37] The identification of external objects, therefore, will depend upon the interpretation of signs given by speaking subjects. But Lacan also accepts the Saussurean point that language is not reducible to the utterances of members of a speech community: these utterances Saussure labelled 'parole'. Saussure's 'langue' is the symbolic system which exists independently of speaking subjects. Having accepted this Saussurean point, Lacan must theorise the relation between this linguistic system and speaking subjects. In order to do this, he introduces a distinction between the 'Other' and the 'other'. The 'other' is the person who appears to me, in my linguistic (and other) communion with her. The Other is that person as she 'truly' is. For example, what I hear you say may not be what you really mean. However, Lacan claims in the end that the real absolutely unattainable 'Other' is language – the symbolic system – itself. We think we have access, in our linguistic communication, to 'language' but in fact all that we are ever acquainted with is the utterances of subjects: *la parole*. *La langue* remains ever inaccessible.

Whereas Freud drew on biology and neurophysiology, Lacan draws on Hegel and structuralism. Yet he accepts some basic Freudian categories. He retheorises the Freudian Oedipus complex. Unlike Freud, however, he has no truck with a biological and developmental account of sexuality. Sexual drives are always analysed by Lacan through the mediation of linguistic processes. Lacan analyses sexuality through the 'discourse' of the analysand in the process of analysis. It is the sexuality about which the analysand talks in which Lacan is interested. Again, like Hegel, and like Rousseau too, Lacan begins this retheorisation with the experience of physical need. He argues that as the child begins to acquire language, so she separates herself from her need. The need is expressed as a demand. But, in the demand, much is left behind, unarticulable and unsatisfiable. One can never, Lacan argues, demand what one really wants. The child, in demanding an object, has focused her pleasure on an imaginary object. Need is largely instinctual; needs are satisfied by the 'consumption' of the object of the need – milk, for example, satisfies the child's hunger. But demands are expressed in language; they take the form 'I want'. Demands are always directed to another: for the child, it will (usually) be the mother. Demand always has two objects – one spoken; the other unspoken. Demand appeals to the other in such a way that, even if the demanded object is given, there can be no satisfaction. This is because the demand is really for something else. The third term, for Lacan, is *desire*. Following Hegel, Lacan describes desire as a fundamental lack – a 'hole' – that can only be satisfied by another's desire. As Hegel argued, each self-conscious subject desires the desire of the other as its object. Desire marks the entry of the child into the symbolic order – the domain of language, sociality and culture. Language, now, has primacy over the subject. Desire, like demand, is in principle insatiable, because the 'other' is the locus of language, law and culture.

This split between need and demand is one aspect of the progress towards humanity. Lacan's rereading of the Oedipal dramas represents another aspect. As Dews puts it:

> The key to [Lacan's] re-interpretation [of Freud] is [his] theory of the phallus, and in this context it is helpful to refer to a passage of [Freud's] 'Inhibitions, Symptoms, Anxiety', where Freud remarks that, 'The high degree of narcissistic value which the penis possesses can appeal to the fact that the organ is a guarantee to its owner that he can be united with his mother – i.e. to a substitute for her – in the act of copulation.'[38]

Dews goes on to explain that Lacan carries this interpretation one stage further by arguing that copulation with the mother is not the real aim of the object; rather 'this is merely an image of full mutual recognition.'[39] The phallus, in other words, symbolises Derridean presence itself, or desire. In reality, for Lacan, as for Derrida, such a signifier is impossible. Lacan theorises this 'loss' of the phallus as castration.

Lacan argues that it is through the realisation of the mother's lack of 'the phallus' that the child first confronts the reality of castration:

> The child experiences the phallus as the centre of the desire of the mother, and situates himself in different positions, through which he is led to deceive this desire: he can identify with the mother, identify with the phallus or present himself as the bearer of the phallus.[40]

Finally, however, the child will have to come to terms with its own symbolic castration. This is equivalent to its full entry into the symbolic order.

The original mother–child relation fails to provide the conditions for full subjecthood. In order for that dynamic mother–child structure to give way to the symbolic order, a third term is required. Lacan argues that it is the paternal symbol – not the real father, but a symbol, 'the phallus' – that represents the power of the law. It is, Grosz argues, the father of Freud's 'Totem and Taboo' – the 'father of individual prehistory' whose death leads to the prohibition of incest. The individual child, then, in order to become a full subject, must introject the name-of-the-father. 'The paternal metaphor ... generates the signification of the subject itself. As a consequence of its operation, the child can represent itself as an "I".'[41] The girl, too, becomes a subject in one sense, yet, in so far as she is positioned as castrated, she is an object of desire for men.

There is, however, another aspect of Lacan's thought which is important for the reading of Irigaray I would like to offer. In addition to the two discourses, the imaginary and symbolic, Lacan refers to a third: the real. This notion is invariably described in relation to the other two. The real, for Lacan, is not the real world, nor is it real experience or intersubjective reality. It is a domain that is unavailable to the subject who exists only in and through symbolic systems. The real appears to be pre-discursive. On the other hand, the real is significant for theorising the subject. In his structuralist phase, the real, for Lacan, is present only through its effects, which are latent in the symbolic realm and are uncovered through psychoanalysis.

In his later work, however, Lacan is more clearly questioning, as Carol Williams has put it, 'the impossible goal of achieving oneness, of recognising the other, of satisfying our desire, of *knowing* the object'.[42] Williams argues that Lacan is here implying that the subject will always remain incomplete and fragmented, and that he is thereby gesturing towards the impossibility of absolute truth and knowledge. She further suggests that the real, at this point, is coded as feminine. As we have already seen, woman, for Lacan, is the missing element in discourse. She is the excluded other, outside grammatical language. 'Woman' enters signification as the 'other' to men. Through this objectification, the masculine subject takes on characteristics of coherence and unity. Woman cannot express her own self, her needs or her pleasures. The real, codified as woman, symbolises, at this stage in Lacan's thinking, the bodily grounding of the masculine self, a self-grounding which precludes the possibility of truth and certainty.

It will be helpful for my reading of Irigaray to highlight some aspects of Lacan's thought which I find problematic.

Some Difficulties Examined

Perhaps the central difficulty with this sketch of some aspects of his theory is that Lacan does not really explain why the phallus is the privileged signifier. We have alluded to the fact that the phallus symbolically represents a mythical state of full recognition by a pair of subjects of one another. But why should it be the phallus that does this? Lacan disclaims any simple connection between 'phallus' and penis: the one is not a device for symbolising the other, so he cannot appeal to the actual penis, or its function or symbolic role, for any part of the explanation. Might there not be other symbols that could fulfil the function of the phallus equally well? Why should not 'Love', for example, a term for a concept that expresses, in some interpretations, full mutual recognition by a pair of subjects, fulfil the appropriate function? Or may there not be other, even better, symbolic devices that would fulfil the role?

One explanation for the position of the phallus Lacan sometimes seems to offer is that it is the father, in many cases, who intervenes to break up the imaginary pre-linguistic unity between mother and child. Thus the 'Law of the Father', the phallus, governs the symbolic order (into which the child enters when he or she leaves the sphere of the 'imaginary'). But this is to appeal to a notion of meaning which Lacan rejects. It is to assume that the phallus represents the father, or his penis, and as we have seen Lacan has distanced himself from a theory of meaning where words refer directly to objects.

In fact, Lacan's thought appears to be contradictory here. On the one hand he disavows any simple connection between words and images or objects, signifiers and signifieds; yet, on the other hand, he makes reference to particular objects in his explanation of the meaning of individual signs. For example, he suggests that the child first experiences castration through seeing the mother's lack of 'the phallus'. But of course she doesn't actually lack 'the phallus'; rather she lacks a penis. Lacan cannot have it both ways. He cannot claim both that the phallus bears no relation to the penis, and also that the child experiences castration (i.e. loss of the phallus) through an awareness of the mother's lack of the penis.

For Lacan, the female subject is always in question, because she lacks the phallus. The symbolic system creates the feminine as absent. However, one wants to ask: why does 'the feminine' feature in the symbolic system in this fashion? Why should 'masculine' signifiers play the role they do in Lacan's system? Isn't he assuming 'phallic' power in his description of the role and function of the phallic signifier? Additionally, Lacan's perspective brings with it further difficulties. If difference is constructed or created by language, then it is not possible to struggle to alter existing inequalities by changing 'real objects' like the family, work relations, etc. Only by constructing a new symbolic system can one begin to chip away at gender inequality. This, indeed, is Irigaray's project.

Irigaray

Irigaray and Psychoanalysis

A central issue for Irigaray is that of psychoanalysis. Throughout her writings (see particularly Whitford, *The Irigaray Reader*) Irigaray deploys psychoanalytic techniques. Yet she is critical of psychoanalysis for a number of reasons. She is sceptical of the power of the analyst: 'interpretation, or merely listening, comes to mean an act which gives the analyst mastery over the analysand, an instrument in the hands of a master and *his* truth.'[43] Psychoanalysis, moreover, operates without acknowledging the historical and philosophical roots of its frame of reference. The text of *Ecrits* (Lacan), for example, functions as a body of eternal truths. Most importantly, however, she argues that psychoanalysis – as received through the texts of Lacan, which is the received currency of non-humanist theoretical analysis in France – is patriarchal. Lacan, like Freud, as we have seen, gives primacy to the phallus. In Irigaray's essay in *Speculum* 'The Blind Spots of an Old Dream of Symmetry' Freud's patrocentric presuppositions are revealed in a series of quotations with ironic commentary. Irigaray suggestively shows how Freud takes the development of the boy as the norm. The girl is therefore a little man (*Speculum*, p. 25). Girls are castrated boys.

On the other hand, Irigaray is steeped in psychoanalysis; she attended Lacan's seminars at the Ecole Normale Supérieure; she was a member of the Ecole Freudienne. She deploys psychoanalytic methods and techniques to investigate the repressed of psychoanalysis and the history of philosophy. She attempts what may be impossible, to move beyond psychoanalytic and classical philosophical presuppositions, by taking up the position of the repressed other, the woman, the feminine. The object of analysis, throughout her writings, is phallocentrism: the Lacanian symbolic order. From a Lacanian starting point, the 'symbolic order' is governed by a recognition of symbolic castration, by 'the law of the phallus'. Yet Irigaray is not operating merely from the 'outside' of the Lacanian symbolic order; rather she sets out to reveal and undermine male bias and the implication of the recognition that the subject is a bodily subject in the history of mainstream thought in general – in the history of philosophy particularly, but also, more recently, in contemporary institutional and political practices. In Lacanian terms, women cannot speak *as* women, because the symbolic order is governed by categories that condemn women to silence. Following on Derrida's insistence, described earlier, and further articulated in *Positions*, that 'the new concept of writing simultaneously provokes the overturning of the entire system attached to it, *and* releases the dissonance of writing within speech, thereby disorganizing the entire inherited order and invading the entire field',[44] Irigaray sets out to discover 'a new concept of the feminine' which would, like Derrida's arché writing, 'overturn the entire system attached to it'. Irigaray denies that she is 'making women the *subject* or the *object* of a theory'.[45] 'The feminine', she says, 'cannot signify itself in any proper meaning, proper name, or concept, not even that of women.'[46]

According to Irigaray, the unsymbolised mother–daughter relation constitutes a potential threat to the patriarchal symbolic order. This relation is the basis for the creation of a symbolic system which Irigaray would suggest subverts the masculine equation of subjectivity with rationality, and acknowledges the bodily roots of subjectivity.

Speculum

Irigaray suggests that the route to a discovery of the feminine and to a subversion of the subject of Enlightenment reason is by 'disrupting'[47] philosophical discourse to reveal its masculinism ('philosophical' includes the work of Freud and Lacan; see *Speculum*, pp. 13–129). 'Disrupting' philosophical discourse occurs in a myriad of ways of which I will mention a few. One example: the text of *Speculum* begins with Freud, it contains sections on Plotinus, Descartes and medieval mysticism in its centre, and it ends with a chapter on Plato's cave metaphor in the *Republic*, thus subverting the order of historical time. But like the quoted sections from Derrida's *Positions*, where 'deconstruction' was said not to involve a simple reversal, so too Irigaray does not simply reverse historical time in the text. Irigaray says of *Speculum* that 'strictly speaking' it has no beginning or end. 'The architectonics of the text, or texts, confounds the linearity of an outline, the teleology of discourse, within which there is no possible place for "the feminine", except the traditional place of the repressed, the censured.'[48] 'Furthermore, by "beginning" with Freud and "ending" with Plato we are already going at history "backwards".' But it is a reversal 'within' which the question of women still cannot be articulated, so this reversal alone does not suffice. That is why, in the book's 'middle' texts – *Speculum*, once again – the reversal seemingly disappears.

'For what is important is to disconcert the staging of representation according to *exclusively* "masculine" parameters.'[49]

Toril Moi suggests that Irigaray's reversal of the historical ordering of the philosophical texts is an action which 'resembles that of the concave mirror which is the speculum gynaecologists use to inspect the "cavities" of the female body'.[50] Moi further points out that the speculum is a male instrument for the penetration of the vagina, but 'it is also a hollow surface, like the one it seeks to explore'.[51] Irigaray uses the technique of imitation or mimicry – mimesis – in her disruption of the philosophical tradition. For example, it is used to undermine the fundamental Freudian and Lacanian device: that of the self-reflection of the subject in the mirror. As we have seen, one central version of Freud's theory of the Ego is a narcissistic one – the self gains a sense of itself through the reflection of the image of his body. The Lacanian self gains an alienated sense of itself as whole and unified through seeing itself in a looking glass. Irigaray mimics the Freudian or Lacanian self looking at himself and reveals the masculinist character of both their lookings. For both see a penis or a 'phallus' when they look. As Nye argues, woman has a vital function, even in 'patriarchal' discourse. She is a blank that 'like a mirror, reflects the masculine'.[52]

Irigaray rejects the Lacanian picture of the subject's formation of itself as a self in the mirror phase. A flat mirror can only be deployed for the masculine subject. Woman, starting from the flat mirror, can only come into focus as the inverted other (mother) of the masculine subject. But the flat, two-dimensional image reflected in the mirror coincides with the use of visual imagery in the history of epistemology. The scopic drive, moreover, is, in psychoanalytic theory, linked to control and domination.

Another example of Irigaray's 'disruption' of philosophical texts is the section of *Speculum* on Plotinus, where she simply presents verbatim a section of his text in order to reveal his masculinism. As Whitford says of this: '[Irigaray] has in mind a kind of "amorous exchange" in which sexual difference would be enacted in language, and she attempts to suggest this textually, to a certain extent, by mingling her own voice with the voice/text of the philosopher.'[53]

In another case, Irigaray disrupts the Enlightenment subject by inserting the woman in mischievous fashion. In the section in *Speculum* on Descartes, 'The Eye of a Man Recently Dead', she says: 'what if the "I" only – thought the thought of a woman.'[54] 'What if I thought only after the other has been inserted, introjected into me? Either as thought or as a mirror in which I reflect and am reflected.'[55] One of the central chapters of *Speculum*, called 'La Mysterique', concerns 'mystic language or discourse'.[56] She says:

This is the place where consciousness is no longer master, where, to its extreme confusion, it sinks into a dark night that is also fire and flames. This is the place where 'she' – and in some cases he, if he follows 'her' lead – speaks about the dazzling glare that comes from the source of light that has been logically repressed, about 'Subject' and 'Other' flowing out into an embrace of fire that mingles one term into another, about contempt for form as such, about mistrust for understanding as an obstacle along the path of the *jouissance* and mistrust for the dry desolation of reason.[57]

The chapter is prefaced by quotations from three medieval mystics – Meister Eckhart, a fourteenth century Dominican who preached to nuns, Angela of Foligno, a fifteenth century saint, and another mystic, Rysbroeck the Admirable. According to Meister Eckhart, 'Woman is the most noble way to address the soul, and it is far nobler than virgin.'[58]

Medieval mystics sought hidden truths or wisdom. Often the mystery of these truths or this wisdom was that they or it couldn't be put into words – some mystics believed wisdom to be attainable by an ecstatic revelation; others thought it was by means of 'intellectual' vision. Mystics often used the marriage/love analogy to talk about the relation between the self and these hidden truths. The soul was said to be feminine.

In her chapter 'La Mysterique', Irigaray suggests that women, who have been 'the poorest in science' have been the most 'eloquent', 'the richest in revelations'.[59] She describes the male 'subject' as 'the one who speaks, sees, thinks, and thereby confers being upon himself',[60] whilst the woman (mystic?) (soul?) goes 'beyond theoretical contemplation'.[61]

Irigaray associates 'women', in this chapter, with 'unreason', 'the unconscious', 'the soul', as with something 'beyond theoretical contemplation'. The chapter appears to be somewhat different from many of the others in *Speculum* where Irigaray is presenting woman as she appears in the eyes of the (male) philosopher whose work she is 'deconstructing'. In the Freud chapter, for example, Irigaray suggestively implies how Freud unwittingly speaks as a man: a woman for him is a man but a castrated one. In the chapter 'Une Mère de Glace' which, as we have seen consists simply of passages, verbatim, from the text of Plotinus *Eneads*, woman is left to speak as Plotinus lets her speak. But in the chapter 'La Mysterique', by contrast, Irigaray speaks positively of the role of women. She appears to associate women with 'unreason', with unconscious madness and with irrationality. It is easy to criticise her, as many have done, by arguing that she is colluding with anti-feminists in celebrating the very qualities of women which have held them in subjection. Perhaps we will come to this conclusion eventually, but we must not do so too quickly.

For we must not forget that Irigaray is a post-Lacanian, post-Derridean thinker. She is spelling out a pre-discursive, corporeal space ignored in

Enlightenment views of the construction of knowledge. Prior to the experience of which we became aware, is the site of 'feminine' desire. Prior to the site of the Lacanian symbolic, the subject's misrecognition of itself in the mirror, is the corporeal space of feminine desire. This could be described as what is 'deconstructed' in the Derridean logocentric self. The Rousseauian child described earlier who both identifies with and desires the mother appeared to be the supreme example of the logocentric self – in Lacanian terms, of the imaginary. And yet Rousseau's text deconstructed itself. The mother, in the Rousseau text, could not satisfy the child's demands for she would have been annihilated if she had. Irigaray could be read as interpolating in here the mother's desire, that intervenes to break up the imaginary unity between mother and child. Irigaray symbolises this as a 'parler-femme' that has been repressed in the masculine symbolic.

Feminine desire could be described as a 'supplement' in Derrida's sense: it is the inessential extra to the 'imaginary' unity between mother and child and to the phallogocentric symbolic. Yet it also reveals what is lacking in the original – it demonstrates that the unity is indeed imaginary and it reveals as illusory the hypothesis that the symbolic realm gives us access to knowledge and certainty.

Some Difficulties

On this particular point, though, I am sceptical. We do not need female desire to tell us that there are difficulties with the claim that certain knowledge of the world is impossible. This claim has been questioned by 'phallocentric' male philosophers as diverse as Hegel, Wittgenstein and Feyerabend (and this is to exclude Derrida and Lacan). Recognition of the presence of the body in knowledge claims surely has to tell us more than this. Furthermore, I remain sceptical about whether this 'parler-femme' can occur. What can we say about the symbolisation of the real that is more than, as Monique Plaza put it, 'the incoherent babblings of a baby'.[62] If, as Cixous says of *l'écriture féminine*, 'it is impossible to *define* a feminine practice of writing ... for the practice can never be theorised, enclosed, encoded,'[63] can anything at all be said about feminine writing, about femininity, about feminine knowledge?

Irigaray's difficulty reflects that of Derrida. As with the latter's attempt to find a route out of the 'logocentric' tradition, so too Irigaray can only escape the symbolic order from an identity acquired in it. She, and indeed anyone else who attempts to travel the same road, is trapped by the fact that the system to be criticised is essential in forming any critique of it. Irigaray self-consciously takes on the question: how can women enter philosophy without contradiction if philosophy is constructed by the exclusion of women? How can philosophy recognise the exclusion of the body? Irigaray's project, indeed, is a recognition of this problem, of the contradiction inherent in what she sets out to do. She says at the end of *Speculum*:

> Precise references in the form of notes or punctuation indicating quotation have often been omitted. Because in relation to the working of theory, the/a woman fulfils a two-fold function – as the mute outside that sustains all systematicity; as a maternal and still silent ground that nourishes all foundations – she does not have to conform to the codes that theory has set up for itself. (p. 365)

The texts, as Whitford puts it so well, 'are dazzling, allusive, deliberately polysemic, difficult to unravel'.[64]

Irigaray does offer positive comment on women by describing their desire: 'woman's desire has doubtless been submerged by the logic that has dominated the West since the time of the Greeks.'[65] 'Within this logic the predominance of the visual, and of the discrimination and individualization of form, is particularly foreign to female eroticism. Woman takes pleasure more from touching than from looking.'[66] Sometimes, however, it appears that when Irigaray comes, in her more political writings, to describe, in more concrete terms, what this celebration of woman's desire amounts to, it is, at least in the short term, to a political separatism.

> But if women are to preserve and expand their autoeroticism, their homosexuality, might not the renunciation of heterosexual pleasure correspond once again to that disconnection from power that is traditionally theirs. For women to undertake tactical strikes, to keep themselves apart from men long enough to learn to defend their desire, especially through speech, to discover the love of other women while sheltered from men's imperious choices and put them in the position of rival commodities, to forge for themselves a social status that compels recognition, to earn their living in order to escape from the condition of prostitute.[67]

These are only stages and Irigaray gives the now familiar Derridean qualification:

> if their aim were simply to reverse the order of things, even supposing this to be possible, history would repeat itself in the long run, would revert to sameness: to phallocratism. It would leave room neither for women's sexuality, nor for women's imaginary, nor for women's language to take (their) place.[68]

But what *would* allow these things to take (their) place?

Irigaray argues that a woman's sexuality is very different from a man's. A man's is instrumental: he must do something to himself. A woman's is autoerotic; she can touch herself. And this, as Nye claims, has consequences.

> Because of this self-touching, there will be no sharp break in her thought between touch and touched, between subject and object. A woman is always in contact with herself; she is both one and at the same time two, contrasted with the male subject which takes things one by one.[69]

This sounds exciting, as though it makes way for a non-logocentric, non-phallocentric form of discourse. At the very least, it appears to allow a form of behaviour where individual subjects, because they 'incorporate' an 'other', take the interests and desires of others into account. She implies that 'patriarchal' societies contain individuals that are fragmented, instrumentalist and individualist. Others, in their ontology, are seen merely as instruments for the satisfaction of one's own needs and desires. Irigaray's own suggested patriarchal ontology is rather akin to a 'collectivist' one, one which takes others as existing, needy, desiring beings in their own right. But Irigaray would not simply be proposing a 'collectivist' versus an individual ontology. Rather, her suggestion would be that the self (the female self) is intrinsically non-individualist; it is 'neither one nor two'. It would not be merely that individuals heed others as independently existing desiring beings, instead the claim would be that the woman's self is intrinsically just as much an 'other' as it is a self. The woman, like the mystic reaching out to God, or the hysteric who has physical symptoms without a physical cause, reaches out to the 'other' because 'the other' is already incorporated inside her. The female self is just as much 'other' as it is a self; the female self is object, like any other object, instead of a 'subject-self'. It gains knowledge of itself in the same way that it acquires knowledge of objects outside itself. It has no special access to itself. Like Merleau-Ponty, Irigaray would be speaking of a 'dual being' ... 'where the other is for me no longer a mere bit of behaviour in my transcendental field, nor I in his: we are collaborates for each other in a consummate reciprocity.'[70] I shall elaborate on this view in Chapter 4.

This might be one interpretation of Irigaray's project. However, she certainly does focus centrally on the importance of developing a new symbolic system in order to overcome women's oppression. The two notions, indeed, are brought together – this symbolic system is to be created as the language of the 'lived body'. As Grosz has put it:

> In analysing how the domination of the right to speak 'universally' has been appropriated by men, Irigaray suggests the procedures

by which the male body is evacuated from or disavowed by phallocentric discourses and signifying practices. In so far as phallocentrism represents itself as disembodied, universal or true, the specific
attributes and interests of men are capable of being presented as
if they were universal. To compensate for this absence of the male
body, women are considered the corporeal, bodily, material sub-
stratum supporting male intellect, reason, theoretical structures –
male immateriality. It is only by reinserting the male body
back into the discourses from which it has been expunged that
femininity and women may be able to establish a discursive space
or position from which to speak (of) their sex.[71]

Irigaray attempts to create a new language for women, by slipping through
the gaps in 'phallic' discourse. The concept 'women' in fact represents for
her 'otherness', that which is 'outside' the phallic specular symbolic system.
In *This Sex which is Not One*, Irigaray suggests that *contra* Freud, the
young girl does know of the existence of her vagina. This primary awareness of her vagina, and of the 'two lips' of her clitoris, Irigaray uses as
a metaphorical device to signify a different kind of language: one that
privileges plurality, instead of the unity of the 'phallic' discourse. The title
of her work expresses both the idea that the woman's sex/gender 'is not
one', that is that it does not exist, and is not one but rather is plural,
multiple. A new 'imaginary', a new 'discourse' would be like the female
genitalia: plural.

One might criticise Irigaray, however, for positing, like the feminist
writer Dale Spender, a 'women's language', that is 'other' than the 'man's
language', and that is ultimately incommensurable with it. A woman's
language that is incommensurable in the radical sense with that of the
man is of doubtful value in the political project of convincing men of
the existence of sexism, and of attempting to alter their behaviour. Does
Irigaray's project suffer in similar fashion? It appears that, unlike Spender,
she is not advocating linguistic separatism. For she is offering a critique
of 'logocentric' discourse, of language that privileges the myth of the
unified Cartesian 'whole' self. Derrida used the neologism 'Différance' to
articulate the rejection of this myth. In this Derridean term, differing is
combined with the idea of deferring, of postponing. Irigaray, in presenting
the language of 'alterity' is not offering us 'women's' language, for, strictly
speaking, there is no 'woman'. Women's essence cannot be characterised.
Woman is always subject to change, and cannot, therefore, be defined.
Instead, therefore, of describing 'women's language', Irigaray offers us
metaphors from female morphology for the new discourse.

I am sceptical, however. As critics of Heraclitus pointed out, long ago,
the fact of change does not make definition impossible. Even if one cannot,
in one sense, step into the same river twice, this does not mean that it is

not possible to identify the river. Even if each woman changes out of all recognition throughout her lifetime, this does not mean that she cannot be identified as the same. She may not be a unified, whole self, but she is, nonetheless, a self, and a self that can be identified as such.

Moreover, even if we grant that there is no 'woman', the problem of incommensurability remains. If the language of the 'other' is not 'phallic' discourse, how does one communicate with those using the latter? Moreover, there are other criticisms we must make of Irigaray's project. As Felman put it (quoted in Moi):

> If 'the woman' is precisely the Other of any conceivable Western theoretical locus of speech, how can the woman as such be speaking in this book? Who is speaking here, and who is asserting the otherness of the woman? If, as Luce Irigaray suggests, the woman's silence or the repression of her capacity to speak, are constitutive of philosophy and of theoretical discourse as such, from what theoretical focus is Luce Irigaray herself speaking in order to develop her own theoretical discourse about women? Is she speaking as a woman, or in the place of the (silent) woman, for the woman, in the name of the woman? Is it enough to be a woman in order to speak as a woman?[72]

It might be argued, however, that these criticisms misunderstand Irigaray's project. Margaret Whitford has argued that Irigaray's aim is not that of stepping right outside the 'male imaginary' – indeed, she suggests that it is not possible to do this. Her project, rather, is 'to psychoanalyse the philosophers',[73] to 'use the methods of the psychoanalyst as an heuristic and epistemological instrument, in an attempt to dismantle the defences of the western cultural unconscious' (p. 33). In her book, Whitford describes two readings of Utopian thinking: one a 'visionary' abstract ideal; the other a metaphor of process. Utopia involves 'the capacity to see afresh'; Utopias are 'operative fantasies' that help change the present. She would locate Irigaray's project inside both senses of Utopia. Irigaray's aim, Whitford explains, is not to step entirely outside the 'symbolic order', but to effect change in it. The process is one of tunnelling from within, bringing about gradual alterations in the machinery of the male imaginary.

Whitford further argues that there are two possible senses of the term 'language' corresponding to the French words 'langue' and 'langage'. The first is 'the corpus of language available to the speaker' and the second 'the corpus as used by a particular person or group, for example, the language of the mentally ill, or the language of lovers' (p. 42). She argues that, when Irigaray talks about developing a different language, it is the latter she has in mind.

These are interesting and illuminating points. I have two reservations
though. First, it is difficult to see how women in general can speak a
common language in Whitford's sense. Irigaray's studies of senile
dementia, in 'Le Langue des Déments' (1973),[74] which revealed sexual
differences in linguistic breakdown, is not sufficient evidence on which to
base a general claim about women's language. Second, the doubt expressed
earlier in relation to Lacan's project remains. Some inequalities between
men and women – e.g. women's receiving lower pay; women's lesser representation in Parliament and in the professions – are real and not symbolic.
It is not clear to me how 'effecting change in the symbolic' can alter this
situation. Moreover, and perhaps more fundamentally, it is unclear to
me exactly what it *means*. Unless one assumes the Lacanian perspective,
it is not obvious that language, or the symbolic, is phallocentric in
the way that Irigaray assumes. I have already made the point that Lacan,
like Freud, appears to take the patriarchal symbolic as a given. If the
metaphorical association of the Lacanian phallus is the father of Freud's
'Totem and Taboo', then, as many critics have pointed out, patriarchy is
assumed and not explained. In that text, which Freud invoked as a
metaphorical anthropological device to 'explain' the power of the Oedipus
complex, the powerful father in the myth controls all women and
children. The sons rise up and destroy the powerful father. But neither
Freud nor Lacan offers any explanation of the father's pre-eminent
position. If the phenomenon is not explained, then it is difficult to see
any way out of it. Moreover, its all pervasive character is questionable.
Only if one accepts the Lacanian story about the origin of self-identity
is phallocentrism as all pervasive as Irigaray and Lacan both take it to
be. The change in standard western childrearing patterns, the variety in
family forms across different countries, the fact that subjecthood changes
and develops throughout life, render the all pervasive character of
Irigaray's and Lacan's view questionable. Irigaray's psychoanalytic
metaphors are precisely that, and, only within this psychoanalytical framework is 'putting us in touch with the mother' an important thing to do.
Reality, surely, is much more messy than the metaphorical framework
assumes. Part of this messiness involves its being less uniformly 'patriarchal' than the metaphor makes it out to be. Reality is both governed by
many more myths and metaphors than Irigaray sometimes assumes and
it is made up of some real structures and relations that are outside these
myths. In the end, the metaphor can tend to function as a straightjacket,
limiting rather than facilitating. Irigaray might be said, then, to be insufficiently postmodernist about symbolic systems.

Some time ago, Toril Moi wrote: 'the material conditions of women's
oppression are spectacularly absent from her [Irigaray's] work.'[75] Moi continues: 'But without specific analysis, a feminist account of power cannot
transcend the simplistic, defeatist vision of male power pulled against female

helplessness that underpins Irigaray's theoretical investigations.'[76] Much has been written about Irigaray since then, but these two key points of criticism – that Irigaray attaches insufficient importance to the 'material' conditions of women's oppression, or, one might add, to 'material' conditions in general; and second, that her analysis of women's oppression is rather more monolithic than is the reality still seem to me to be valid.

Moi argues, moreover, that Irigaray contradicts her own prescription, in her practice. Her 'prescription' is frequently for a mimicry of male discourses. But, Moi argues, often in fact she falls, despite herself, into a 'logocentric' style of writing. She argues that Irigaray's essay 'Le Marche des Femmes' (in *This Sex*, pp. 165–185), where Irigaray uses Marx's categories to 'criticise' patriarchy, turns out to be a vindication of Marx's categories, rather than a disruption of them.

Furthermore, there may be difficulties with Irigaray's project which are analogous to some criticisms of early versions of feminist standpoint theory. The feminist epistemologist, Sandra Harding, has pointed out that there are fundamental similarities between early versions of feminist standpoint theory (the theory that there is a specifically woman's epistemological standpoint) (see Chapter 5) and epistemological theories offered by, for example, African 'others' so that it is difficult to see why these theories should be described, specifically, as theories of a *woman's* standpoint.[77] What guarantee is there that there is not a similar difficulty here? What guarantee do we have that the creation of a feminine symbolic system will not form either the 'oppressor' system relative to black people or people with disabilities, to take two possible groupings, or that the female symbolic is not precisely analogous to an African symbolic? In either of these two events, there would be no ground for the association of the 'feminine' symbolic with a *feminist* project. In the former instance, 'feminism', far from being radical, would be itself a form of domination; and, in the latter instance, there would be no better grounds for labelling it the symbolic of 'the other': it would be that of *anyone* who is 'other' to the dominant symbolic.

But there are more fundamental difficulties, I believe, with Irigaray's project, than any so far mentioned. Derrida, Lacan and Irigaray have in common a preoccupation with the relation of language and meaning to subjectivity and consciousness. Although Derrida, Lacan and Irigaray are critical of Saussure, nonetheless they all accept some version of the Saussurean structuralist point that the relation between signifier and signified is arbitrary and that signifiers gain their meaning through their differential relations with other signifiers, rather than through any direct link with the signified. Despite her refusal to ally herself either with Derrida or with Lacan, she depends partially upon their acceptance of the Saussurean view of meaning. I believe this theory of meaning to be mistaken. In the following chapter, I will explain why.

3
Realism and Anti-Realism

Realism

Postmodern theorists, following their structuralist predecessors, have been critical of 'realism' in the theory of meaning. Many of them pursue, and elaborate upon, the structuralism of Saussure. In this chapter, I would like to offer a defence of an unfashionable realist approach to meaning. I will go on, in the latter part of the chapter, to explain how a number of postmodernist/poststructuralist theorists are anti-realist and I will describe what I believe is left out of their theories, by virtue of their anti-realism. This chapter explores further my disagreement with Irigaray.

Several theorists, at certain points in their histories, have described themselves as 'realists'. Amongst them are Hilary Putnam, Roy Bhaskar and John Koethe. Each of these thinkers has described himself as a 'metaphysical realist'.

Superficially, metaphysical realism is a theory of knowledge and truth: it is a theory which separates out the conditions for the truth of a theory from the conditions for its verification. As Koethe has graphically put it: 'we might be "brains in a vat" and so the theory that is "ideal" from the point of view of operational utility, inner beauty and elegance, "plausibility", "simplicity", "conservatism", etc. "might be false". "Verified" does not imply true.'[1] The concept of truth becomes transcendent of anyone's knowledge: the truth or falsity of any sentence may be independent of the conditions for its verification. The world and a true description of it may be different from the best possible verified theory. A sentence, indeed, may be understood, although there can be no possible recognition of the circumstances which would fulfil its truth conditions.

The view of another realist, Roy Bhaskar, is slightly different in emphasis. Bhaskar describes himself both as a 'metaphysical' and as a 'transcendental' realist. According to him, 'realism is the theory that the ultimate objects of scientific inquiry exist and act (for the most part) quite independently of scientists and their activity.'[2] For him, realism is crucially not a theory of truth or knowledge, but of *being*: it is of crucial importance that statements about being are not reducible to statements about anyone's knowledge of being.

Bhaskar accepts that any theory of knowledge presupposes some view of what the world must be like. Empiricist theories, for example, presuppose an ontology to the effect that the objects of knowledge are the objects either of actual or possible experience. However, Bhaskar goes further than this. He argues that the intelligibility of experimental work in the sciences presupposes a stronger ontology: 'an ontology of real things and structures, events and possibilities of the world; and for the most part they are quite independent of us.'[3] Bhaskar wrote this before his interest moved from the natural to the social sciences, and he would now include amongst these 'real things' social structures – for instance, the economy, the state, the family and language all of which depend upon or presuppose social relations. He believes that social structures and social relations pre-exist the individuals who enter into them and yet he suggests that social theory and social reality are causally independent.

Bhaskar continues to hold, however, that the ontological field is richer than patterns of events produced by scientists. These events, he argues, enable scientists to identify the mode of operation of structures, mechanisms or processes which they do not produce. Bhaskar argues that these structures, and the causal laws which describe their *modus operandi*, would exist in a world without human beings. Presumably Bhaskar would actually wish to modify this claim to the view that *some* of these structures would exist in such circumstances, since some of the social structures depend crucially on the existence of human beings. However, the point he wishes to emphasise is the relative independence of real structures and processes, both from scientific theories and from individual and collective *experience*. A further important point he wants to make is the possibility of a non-human world that would operate even if it were unknown. This is a viewpoint shared by the realist Putnam, for whom there is a possibility that any humanly produced theory may fail to describe the nature of the real world, and for whom, therefore, this world might operate quite independently of human beings.

This chapter offers a defence of realism. Feminism will not be at the forefront of my discussion, but the arguments form part of my disagreement with postmodernist influenced feminism, and of the discussion that will follow in later chapters.

Rorty

Realist theorists have come in for critical scrutiny from a range of quarters – notably from contemporary French theorists. But one of the best known 'analytical' philosophical critics of such theories is Richard Rorty. In *Philosophy and the Mirror of Nature*, he questions realism. He illustrates the way in which 'realism' in philosophy of language and philosophy of science fits with the epistemological perspective he rejects. His task, in that book, is to criticise 'foundationalist' theories of knowledge; and to suggest that, instead, philosophy should be seen to be a 'cultural genre', 'a voice in the conversation of mankind'.[4] He spends some time articulating the view that 'traditional philosophy' is held captive by the idea of the mind mirroring or representing the world.[5] His first task is to question the notion of 'the mind' – his argument is that the concept philosophers take for granted is in fact their invention; and that foundationalism in epistemology – the attempt to ground knowledge in certain foundations – flows from this myth. The central criterion of the mental is indubitability; knowledge then consists in moving from the mental to the physical realms – using the former to *represent* the latter. By this process – since the criterion for the mental is indubitability – one thereby sets out to refute the sceptic about the existence of the external world. His view, however, is that this cannot be done, and the whole 'foundationalist' project is a myth. In the chapter 'Philosophy of Language', he argues that recent theories of language, notably 'realism' and theories of reference, merely perpetuate this fiction. He is at pains to point out, however, that the philosophy of language of Donald Davidson lies in a different trajectory from the objectionable foundationalist epistemology. Davidson constantly denies that he is *analysing* meaning: in his view, the question of 'how knowledge works' has no special connection with the question of 'how language works'.[6] For Davidson, a theory of meaning 'provides an understanding of the inferential relations between sentences'.[7]

It is rather on the work of Davidson's critics – notably, Putnam and Dummett, who do see a crucial link between epistemological questions and issues in the theory of meaning – that Rorty focuses. He considers particularly questions about theory change in science. In his view, 'we' do not usually suppose that questions like 'Do the Neuer refer to the soul as *kwoth*?' can be answered by matching 'one-word expressions' in one culture by 'one-word expressions' in another. However, questions like 'Was Aristotle wrong about motion being divided into natural and forced? or was he talking about something different from what we talk about when we talk about motion?' do seem vitally important to us.

He points out that one possible answer – the idea that people are 'really talking about' the essence of a thing, characterised by the analytic statements telling one the meaning of the term for the thing (versus the synthetic statements which express possible false beliefs about the object) – has been undermined by Quine's article 'Two Dogmas of Empiricism'. In his famous article Quine argued that the distinction between analytic and synthetic statements is not a distinction of kind. Acceptance of Quine's point, therefore, meant that philosophers had to look elsewhere for the solution. They began looking, Rorty points out, to the theory of reference and a 'realistic' philosophy of science.

Rorty then examines Putnam's version of realism. He considers that there is only one of Putnam's arguments which he need take really seriously. He believes that Putnam's point, put earlier, that 'true theory' may not mean the same thing as 'best possible verified theory' is acceptable, but that it need not establish realism because we have no grounds for hypostatising anything at all outside the domain of the best possible verified theory. Another point made by Putnam in favour of realism – that scientific theories tend to converge – Rorty thinks, again, does not establish realism. It is perfectly possible, after all, that they converged for other reasons than that the independently existing real world just happened to be that way.

It is on another of Putnam's arguments that Rorty directs his more considered attention. Putnam, in his realist phase, agreed that we should not accept a theory which compels us to draw the conclusion that electrons are just like phlogiston. The word 'electron', Putnam argues, refers to a real entity – the electron – whereas the word 'phlogiston' did not. It is unacceptable, Putnam argues, for us to hold anti-realist theory which does not allow us to draw the distinction between words which really refer and those which do not. Rorty has a rejoinder to this, however. He objects strongly to the notion of reference. He argues that the concept 'reference' is a spurious concept that results from running together two considerations:

> The fact, noted by Kripke, Donnellon and others, that there are counterexamples to the Searle-Strawson criterion for reference – that is, that S refers, in his use of 'x' to whatever entity would make most of his central beliefs about x true.

> The fact that the usual [Frege, Strawson, Searle] assumption that meaning, in the sense of beliefs or intentions (or, more generally, entities in the heads of users of words) determines reference suggests that the more false beliefs we have, the less 'in touch with the world' we are.[8]

In other words, Rorty is arguing that the expression 'x refers' is a confused expression that has been used in two quite different ways: on the one hand it has been used to mean the following: 'x picks out a really existent object y'. On the other hand, however, it has been used to mean 'x picks out a non-existent entity' in cases where 'what makes most of someone's beliefs about x true' happens to be something that, in fact, does not actually exist. So, Rorty argues, the theory of reference is hopelessly confused:

> I think, then, that the quest for a theory of reference represents a confusion between the hopeless 'generic' quest for a general theory of what people are 'really talking about' and the equally hopeless 'epistemological' quest for a way of refuting the sceptic and underwriting our claim to be talking about non-fictions.[9]

The theory of reference, then, according to Rorty, cannot be used to mediate in the discussion between the realist and the non-realist, since it is itself bound up with two theories – epistemological attempts to refute the sceptic, on the one hand, and attempts to establish what people are 'really' talking about – both of which, Rorty believes, are misguided.

It is important to point out, however, that whilst this may be an effective argument against the use of the notion of reference as a weapon in the battle against foundationalist versions of realism, it is not necessarily effective against Bhaskar's 'transcendental' realism nor is it effective against all notions of reference. Bhaskar, himself, is as vehemently critical of mind/body dualism and 'foundationalism' as Rorty. So Rorty's argument that there is an intrinsic connection between foundationalism and realism is not correct. One could continue to believe in reference in the sense of words picking out something in the world independent of us, without the foundational trappings. Bhaskar himself has said, of Rorty, that he tends to presuppose that *any* epistemology must be foundationalist and empirical. He seems to suggest, in other words, that the only realist epistemology there is is one that sets out to offer a 'God's eye' view of the world, rather like that of Wittgenstein in the *Tractatus*, where true sentences perfectly 'picture' states of affairs in the world. But one can, however, believe in a world where one can sometimes refer to objects outside oneself without taking this on board.

Bhaskar has, himself, argued against Rorty that 'the crucial questions in philosophy are not whether to be a realist or anti-realist, but *what sort of* realist to be (an empirical, conceptual, transcendental, or whatever, realist)'. He continues: 'While arguing that we never encounter reality *except under a chosen description*, Rorty unwittingly imbibes and inherits Hume's and Kant's chosen descriptions of the reality known by the sciences.'[10]

I have reservations, therefore, about Rorty's critiques of realism. But how might one support the position?

Some Support for 'Metaphysical Realism'

One argument in favour of 'metaphysical realism' is the following: unless real structures and processes existed independently of scientific theorists, experimentation would make no sense. To carry out an experiment, you need something on which to do so. Both Roy Bhaskar and Gaston Bachelard, in slightly different ways, have made this point.[11] If this point is not made, it would appear that knowledges are produced *ex nihilo*. Second, the hypothetical entities and mechanisms presupposed for the purposes of theory construction must themselves derive part of their meaning from some other source, or the process of theory construction would itself make no sense. Third, the phenomenon of incommensurability – where the same expression in two different theories has a radically different sense – could not be described unless there is something extraneous to each theory over which the two theories clash. It is not possible, in other words, to say of two theories that they clash, unless there is something over which they can be said to disagree. But there is, fourthly, an argument of a different kind. The point is sometimes made in the theory of quantification that the range of a sentence of the form 'All x's' is actually a denumerable infinity of individuals. The 'verification' condition for such a sentence would be a denumerable infinity of individuals. However, it is said, it is impossible for anyone ever to establish that these conditions obtain. We must, therefore, distinguish the conditions for the truth of such a sentence from the conditions that we could deploy to verify it.[12]

I believe, therefore, that there are some good reasons, Rorty notwithstanding, for upholding realism. In the remainder of this chapter, I would like to spell out some anti-realist aspects of the thought of Derrida, Lacan and Irigaray and some points a realist might make about their thinking.

Derrida, Lacan and Irigaray and Anti-Realism

I begin this discussion with Derrida. This time I will refer primarily to those sections of *Of Grammatology* where Derrida discusses Saussure. It would be useful to preface this discussion by looking at some of the writings of Saussure himself.

In his *Course in General Linguistics*,[13] Saussure argues, famously, that languages are constituted by internal relations. He claims that we cannot define phonemes in terms of their acoustic properties – the physical properties of the sound wave. There are at least two reasons why this is so. First of all, individual phonemes occurring in one place in a word sound different from their occurrences elsewhere in the word: 't' at the beginning of the word 'table', for example, sounds different from 't' in the word 'utter'. Secondly, there are enormous variations in the way words sound amongst speakers.

Saussure claimed that the linguistic system itself determines the amount of variation that is permitted. The linguistic system brings it about that certain differences between sounds are important – that some announce a change in sign. Saussure extended this idea to the syntactic and semantic aspects of language. He claimed that the linguistic contribution of each item to the language is given by its differences from other 'bits' of the language: 'each linguistic term derives its value from its opposition to all other terms.'[14] Saussure avers that all the relationships (syntagmatic* and paradigmatic*) into which each term enters with every other contribute to determining its meaning. Furthermore, these relations *exhaust* the meaning of each word. For example, there is nothing more to the meaning of the word 'black' than its relations with other signs. Already we see one respect in which Saussure is an anti-realist. He denies that reference plays any role at all in the meaning of any word. The meaning of the word 'black' is exhausted by its relations with other signs.

Saussure does distinguish the signified (that which is signified) from the signifier (that which signifies). But this signified is not a language-independent referent – rather it is a concept, a thought. Moreover, the nature of this thought is determined by relations internal to the language.

I would argue, however, with the realist, that reference is crucial to capturing the difference between language, which is used to communicate, and games, like chess. The rules of chess are internal to the game, and the moves in the game occur solely in it. Although Saussure would have us believe otherwise, this is not the case with language. And there are difficulties consequent upon the rejection of reference. It becomes difficult to explain developmental facts about language. Any new term introduced into the language will change the meaning of all other terms. How then will language acquisition take place? One of Saussure's reasons for rejecting reference is that he argues that linguistic signs are *arbitrary*. There is no intrinsic relation between the sign 'dog' and dogs; the word 'dog' has no dog-like qualities. Therefore, according to him, the meaning of the word 'dog' is wholly defined by its relations with other words.

Derrida and Saussure

This 'arbitrariness' of the sign is something of which Derrida approves in Saussure. He quotes, without obvious disagreement, 'the thesis of the *arbitrariness* of the sign'.[15] Where Derrida 'disagrees' with Saussure (and I use this expression recognising that it is not one of which Derrida would

---

* Syntagmatic relations are those a word holds to other words, with which it can be joined in strings, for instance 'Alison' and 'laughs': these two can be joined to form a sentence; whilst paradigmatic relations are those a word holds to others that could be substituted for it in the well formed unit.

approve) is not here, but elsewhere. He approves of Saussure's views on the relationality of linguistic terms. But he thinks that Saussure did not go far enough. Saussure, Derrida points out, 'contests' the notion that speech 'clothes' thought.[16] Speech, Derrida is saying, for Saussure, does not represent thought. Individual spoken words do not name or refer to thoughts. Instead, as we have seen, thoughts for Saussure only exist in language. Language creates thought. But, Derrida says, Saussure continues to uphold the 'old', 'logocentric' view on the relation between speech and writing. Writing, for Saussure, as with the philosophers in the logocentric tradition before him – Plato, Aristotle, Rousseau and Hegel, to name but a few – is derivative of speech.

Writing, for Saussure, according to Derrida, is 'artificial exteriority', a 'clothing' of speech.[17] Writing represents speech. Saussure, just like his predecessors, mistakenly, says Derrida, takes the spoken word to be the object of linguistics.[18] Writing will be 'the outside, the exterior representation of language and of this "thought-sound" '.[19] Writing, therefore, says Derrida, is the sign of a sign. Derrida is claiming, in other words, that Saussure ought to have extended his thesis about the meanings of signs to the relation between writing and speech. Just as each internal sign gains its meaning from its relations to other signs, and just as thought is nothing over and above the relations between these signs, so should writing be. Writing ought to be itself nothing but the relations between linguistic signs. But, Derrida would say, once one sees the relation between speech and writing in this fashion, then the distinction between speech and writing is undermined altogether. Speech becomes a form of writing, and writing a type of speech.

Although Saussure, therefore, according to Derrida, removes himself from the logocentric tradition with his view on the arbitrariness of the sign, he nonetheless remains caught up in it as regards his perspective on speech and writing.

Derrida is 'objecting' then to another aspect of realism. He concurs with Saussure's rejection of the notion of reference, and further with his perspective on the relation between language and thought, but he adds one further dimension – the rejection of the distinction between speech and writing.

Saussure sees a connection between the view that the relation between a term and the object for which it stands is *arbitrary*, and the claim that the meaning of every term is given by its relations to all others. Saussure argues that it is *because* the meanings of signs are arbitrary that there is no reference. But it could be the case both that the arbitrariness claim holds *and* that signs refer. Reference does not depend on signs being like their referents. Derrida, in bringing his accusation of logocentrism against so many writers in the history of philosophy, sometimes writes as though it does. Derrida gives the following characterisation of the logocentric philosopher:

if, for Aristotle, for example, 'spoken words are the symbols of mental experience and written words are the symbols of spoken words' (Aristotle, *De Interpretatione*), it is because the voice, producer of *the first symbols*, has a relationship of essential and immediate proximity with the mind. Producer of the first signifier, it is not just a simple signifier among others. It signifies 'mental experiences' which themselves reflect or mirror things by natural resemblance.[20]

Derrida is describing Aristotle, but one has a sneaking suspicion that this may be his model for logocentrism in general.

So far, in characterising Derrida's views on language, I have referred solely to *Of Grammatology*. Yet his anti-realism is clearly articulated throughout the corpus of his writings. In 'Structure, Sign and Play', for example, in *Writing and Difference*,[21] Derrida says, in Saussurean vein:

[this was] the moment when, in the absence of a center or origin, everything became discourse – provided we can agree on this word – that is to say, a system in which the central signified, the original or transcendental signified, is never absolutely present outside a system of differences.[22]

Derrida refers approvingly, in this paper, to Nietzsche and Freud: the former because of his 'critique of metaphysics', 'the critique of the concepts of Being and truth, for which were substituted the concepts of play, interpretation, and sign (sign without present truth)', and Freud for his 'critique of self presence, that is the critique of consciousness, of the subject, of self-identity and self-proximity or self-possession'; and, more radically, he says, 'the Heideggerian destruction of metaphysics, of ontotheology, of the determination of Being as presence'.[23]

As we have already seen, in the quote from *Of Grammatology*, the model of meaning of which Derrida 'disapproves' is one which has the meanings of words like Lockean ideas 'present' in the mind of the speaker as she utters the word. But, this need not be the perspective on meaning held by the realist. Not all those who believe in reference are like Descartes or Locke. As Callinicos has put it: '[Derrida's position] finds its roots in – Heidegger aside – a philosophy of language which moves from the rejection of the atomistic theories of meaning typical of 17th Century epistemology to the denial of any relation of discourse to reality.'[24]

Throughout his writings, from the very early *Origin of Geometry* to recent works, we find the view of meaning affirmed. In *Glas* and in *Positions* (where Derrida summarises his main concerns in a very clear fashion) the preoccupation with the arbitrariness of the sign, and with the extension of this to the relation between speech and writing, remains.[25]

Lacan

We find a similar perspective articulated in Lacan. Peter Dews, in his book *The Logics of Disintegration*, describes a shift in Lacan's thought that took place after the writing of the *Discours de Rome*. This change, he says, 'was undoubtedly in large part the result of a growing awareness of the methodological principles of structuralism'.[26]

As Dews points out, Lacan's early writings contain material which provides fertile ground for the acceptance of structuralist ideas. There is a 'strain of argument', he suggests, in 'De la Psychose Paranoiaque dans ses Rapports avec la Personnalité' where Lacan is 'anxious to deny that a semantic and psychogenic account of mental illness must entail the ruin of scientific objectivity'.[27]

In the later works, however, the debt to Saussure is much more clearly apparent. Lacan accepts the Saussurean perspective on the arbitrariness of the relation between signifier and signified. This Saussurean claim, for Lacan, in 'Function and Field of Speech and Language' is important in so far as it discourages, he believes, a misleading, imaginary identification with 'the other'.[28] We have seen how Lacan sees all self-consciousness, all self-identification as illusory. His suggestion is that a non-Saussurean conception of the relation between signifier and signified acts as a metaphor for an identification with the other, or with a perspective according to which one identifies with one's reflection in the mirror.

Once again we have a thinker associating non-structuralist, non-Saussurean views on meaning with a non-arbitrary connection between signifier and signified. In Lacan's case this link with the visual, specular imagery is clear-cut. He reverses the metaphorical connection between mirror symbolism and language. Instead of the mirror symbolism acting as a metaphor for meaning, things are the other way about. Yet he shares with other anti-realists the perspective on realism whereby signifiers picture/mirror their referents. But, as we have seen, this may be a mis-leading characterisation of realism.

Furthermore, again like Derrida, Lacan accepts that one can study language independently of its referents. 'The signifier [he says] has its own laws, independent of the signified.'[29] In other words, Lacan accepts the Saussurean point that language is like chess; one can study its rules and its operations, independent of its function of referring to the real world. But language, I have argued, is not like chess.

The interpretation of signs, for Lacan, as with Saussure, depends on their interconnection with all other signs: 'in that structure each element assumes its precise function by being different from the others' and 'signi-fication is realised only on the basis of a grasp of things in their totality.'[30] No act of reference can take place independent of language as a whole.

But it is surely partly this Saussurean perspective on language which leads Lacan to the view that: 'speech is moving towards nothing less than a transformation of the subject to whom it is addressed.'[31] He gives his famous example: the statement 'you are my wife' bestows that new reality on its addressee. The individual becomes wife by being addressed that way. This is an anti-realist aspect of Lacan's thought. Lacan is extending the consequence we noted earlier of Saussurean linguistics, whereby each new linguistic acquisition alters the language as a whole, to the relation between language and reality. Because, in the Lacanian system, the language – the speech patterns, the Saussurean *parole* – creates reality, it does so on each occasion the subject uses it.

A further aspect of Lacan's structuralism and his anti-realism occurs in his attitude towards the past. Analysis, according to him, is not a reliving of the past, but a 'reconstruction' of it: 'It is less a question of remembering than of rewriting history.'[32]

Analysis, therefore, is not concerned with discovering 'facts' about the life history of the patient. All one has to go on, after all, in analysis is: 'the patient's speech'.[33]

I accept that in the matter of the unconscious and of fantasy 'truth' may be a misleading epithet. Yet it is not just in this realm, as we have seen, that Lacan is an anti-realist. His anti-realism expresses itself in many facets of his thought.

One final area is that, for Lacan, the symbolic system determines individual subjectivity. There is no subjectivity outside language. There can be no thoughts independently of language. The analyst, Lacan says, must not uncover an 'imaginary intention' from 'the symbolic relation in which it is expressed'.[34] 'Nothing must be read into it [the symbolic expression] concerning the ego of the subject.'[35] Now while it is true that thoughts – beliefs, intentions, etc. – are formulated in language, the realist might argue that one can have some thoughts without being in possession of the word for those thoughts.

Irigaray

There are many aspects of Irigaray's thought, as well, which make her an anti-realist. She suggests that 'the feminine cannot signify itself in any proper meaning, proper name, or concept, not even that of women.'[36] She denies that she 'is making women the *subject* or the *object* of a theory'.[37] In other words, like Derrida and like Lacan, she rejects *reference*. The term 'woman' does not, according to her, gain any part of its meaning from referring to women. Its meaning, rather, like Saussure's terms, derives from its place in language – its place, specifically, in two discourses: feminine language and 'phallocentric' discourse. As we have seen, feminine language can only be hinted at, in mimicry and metaphor. The mystic speaks it, and so does the hysteric. It is a language rich in revelations, but poor in devices enabling reasoning to take place. One might never arrive at a specification of the meaning of any term in this language, for, as we have seen, it is possible we can say nothing about it more than 'the incoherent babblings of a baby'. This language is in direct contrast with the language Irigaray describes as 'phallogocentric' discourse.

Irigaray's 'feminine' language may be incommensurable with the 'male' language of reason in analogous fashion to the discourses of Einstein and Newton, for Feyerabend. For the latter, the term 'mass' in the two outlooks is utterly different in meaning. The two men occupy different realities. Men and women, for Irigaray too, may live in different worlds, speak in ways that are incomprehensible to one another. The realist, however, views things differently. She does not take the partial variation in senses of terms like 'mass' in any two theories to indicate a difference in reference. Reference, and the world, remain constant in any alteration of theory. Thus had Irigaray been a realist she would not have spoken of developing different *languages* or occupying radically disparate realities. A realist Irigaray would have recognised that there must be some commonality of sense between the language of the 'masculinist' and that of the feminist. The realist would say, moreover, that only if this is the case can one hope to bring about changes in *reality*. Sexism, she would contend, is a real phenomenon, existing in the real world, and is not confined to language. In her essay on Freud, 'The Blind Spot of an Old Dream of Symmetry', in *Speculum*, the real Irigaray concurs with Freud (whom she has just quoted):

> One can only agree in passing that it is impossible exhaustively to represent what women might be, given that a certain economy of representation – inadequately perceived by psychoanalysis, at least in the 'scientific discourse' that it speaks – functions through a tribute to woman that is never paid or even assessed. The whole problematic of Being has been elaborated thanks to that loan. It is thus, in all exactitude, unrealisable to describe the being of woman.[38]

Woman is represented as 'other' in the language of phallocentrism. Therefore, according to Irigaray, one cannot (except in mystic discourse) describe her at all. But the realist would intervene here, and proclaim that even if it is true that woman is 'absent' from certain forms of representation, the term 'woman' is not 'absent' in language. Although the sense given to the term in the Freudian corpus Irigaray is examining may be such as to render her invisible in Freudian theory, or in Platonic theory, she is *not* absent from language. Women and the feminine are not even absent from Freud's writings: Irigaray herself quotes a myriad of occurrences of the terms. What is absent from Freud's discourses is a

sense for the terms 'feminine' and 'woman' which valorises women positively. The appropriate response to Freud, I would suggest, in realist vein,
is not to renounce altogether 'the language of masculinism', but to retain
the term 'woman', part of the sense of which is to refer to real women,
and alter its meaning. As Mary Daly suggests, certain terms should be
revalorised, from a feminist perspective (not a *feminine* one). This should
not, now *contra* Daly, lead to the conclusion that there is a separate
female *language*, rather it ought to lead one to think that some men have
previously been using these terms *about women* wrongly. Really women
are not as Freud characterises them. Part of the sense of the term 'woman',
in Freudian theory, then, is wrong.

One aspect of Irigaray's anti-realism can be uncovered, therefore, by
looking at her views on 'phallocentrism' in language. But Irigaray is also
like Derrida and like Lacan, I believe, in her perspective on 'phallocentric'
discourse. Like her predecessors, she associates the view that there is reference in language with its analogue in the theory of Cartesian self-certainty
– the quasi Lockean view that words are direct symbols of mental
experience. When she denounces the phallocentrism of the philosophical
tradition, this is ultimately what she has in mind. Throughout her writings Irigaray associates masculinity with visual symbols, and particularly
with the adopting of subject position in mirror symbolism. This occurs
most starkly in her piece on Descartes in *Speculum*, 'The Eye of a Man
Recently Dead', but we see it elsewhere. Female nature, in the tradition,
she says, is characterised by lack, and a lack of something visible. When
the Freudian or Lacanian little girl looks in the mirror, since the focus
of her looking is supposed to be the penis, she sees nothing. Thus, when
she looks, there is nothing to see. Woman is what the masculine man is
not: she becomes associated with qualities the masculine man either does
not possess, or that he seeks to transcend: the womb, the earth, matter,
receptacle, or in the Freudian case – nothing.

The metaphor, in language, that underlies all of this, is the Lockean one.
Words 'mirror' or 'picture' things, in this perspective, as well as picturing
or mirroring their senses. The relation between words, objects and concepts
is analogous to the relation between the Cartesian self – the thinking
self – and the cogito, the 'I think'. Irigaray calls it 'the specular makeup
of discourse, that is, the self-reflecting (stratifiable) organization of the subject in that discourse'.[39] But this model of language, to reiterate once more,
is not the only one there is for the 'phallocrat' (or for the feminist, what
is more) who believes in realism and in reference in language.

Concluding Remarks

Contrary to Derrida's perspective, one can believe in reference, without
being a strict 'logocentric' philosopher. Furthermore, one could happily

be a feminist critic of Freud without accepting that there are two languages. In other words, one does not have to believe, as all three thinkers appear to hold that one must, that the meaning of the word 'table' is exhausted by its picking out the object in question, in order to uphold a referential element in linguistic terms. Similarly, referential theorists of meaning need not be strict adherents to the 'metaphysics-of-presence': they need not claim that referential terms are like the Cartesian 'I' in 'I think'; referential terms are not 'present-to-themselves' in the way that the 'I' is, for Descartes, in the act of thinking. There is, therefore, a position – indeed probably several – intermediate between the 'metaphysics-of-presence' and 'difference' or 'feminine' language. One does not have to deny *all* reference in denying the metaphysics-of-presence.

In the next chapter I am going to move into a different area of discussion – I shall be looking at the views of Irigaray and others on the subject of knowledge. Those who are more interested in reading about a feminist epistemology that is compatible with the realism defended here should move straight to Chapter 5.

4
Irigaray and the Self

In the previous chapter I looked at one theme in poststructuralist/post-modern thought – the theory of meaning. In this chapter, I propose to look, focusing again partly on Irigaray, at the conception of the subject.

Many contemporary thinkers who have analysed the 'crisis of modernity' have challenged the notion of the unitary self. Psychoanalytic thinking – both Freudian and Lacanian – stresses that the recognition of the role of the unconscious explodes the notion of a whole, unitary self. Recent French writing, ranging from the Marxism of Althusser, through Foucault, Derrida and Deleuze, all emphasises, from very different perspectives, what Derrida, in *Margins of Philosophy*, has described as 'the end of man'.[1] In this chapter I would like to look critically at this view.

Irigaray argues that the unitary humanist subject is a construction of 'phallocentrism'. She suggests that woman violates the ontological condition of the unitary subject. Woman is 'neither one nor two'. This is despite the fact that, as Margaret Whitford has put it, 'the question of female subjectivity is *central* to Irigaray's work'.[2] The creation of women's 'language' is a condition of their coming-to-be a subject. At the moment, Whitford argues, Irigaray situates women in object position; 'in language they are the predicate'.[3] Irigaray's task is for women to come to occupy subject position.

In much of her writing, Irigaray attempts to speak as though the presupposition of a unitary self were not operating. Thus, she subverts the linearity of time; she mingles her own voice with that of the person about whom she is writing; she adopts the metaphor of the fluid, as distinct from the presupposition of a singular, continuous *solid* subject. These metaphors, however, are all taken to be metaphors that flow from the attempt (fatally flawed as it might be) to 'speak as a woman'. She suggests that the metaphor of the unitary, solid subject is inapplicable to women, since, unlike the man, who has to touch 'his sex' externally with his hand, the woman 'touches herself' all the time, and moreover, no-one can forbid her to do so, for her genitals are formed of two lips in continuous contact. Thus, within herself, she is already two – but not divisible into one(s) – 'that caress each other'.[4]

In the 'male imaginary' that has, according to Irigaray, 'dominated the West since the time of the Greeks',[5] 'discrimination and individualisation of form' has occurred. Women, however, take pleasure more from touching than looking; she 'is neither one nor two'.[6] 'Rigorously speaking, she can neither be represented as one person, nor as two. She resists all adequate definition. Woman, in cultural systems that prioritise the notion of ownership, is object of exchange. Women are traditionally use-value for men; they are wives, mothers. They are products.'[7] Inheritance, invariably in these cultures, passes through the male line. 'Ownership and property', Irigaray claims, 'are doubtless quite foreign to the feminine.'[8]

I emphasised in Chapter 2 Irigaray's preoccupation with psychoanalytic theory. One reason for this preoccupation is that psychoanalytic theory attempts a 'science of sex', and yet Freudian theory often fails to recognise that there are two sexes.[9] But additionally, it is psychoanalytic theory that performs two important tasks. First, it provides an account of the way in which individuals become human; an explanation of the way in which 'the mass of uncoordinated limbs', to borrow a Lacanian phrase, takes on an identity (though illusory) as a self-conscious subject. And second, it purports to explain how individuals become gendered selves. Thus, for those cultures that take individuality to be so important, psychoanalysis is pivotal (even though this pivotal character may go unrecognised by many). For Irigaray, then, psychoanalysis is the theory *par excellence* that accounts for the purported subjecthood of the male, and confines the woman to 'other' or 'object'. In Freudian theory, compared to the boy, the girl 'has no sex'.[10] She has few of the qualities that characterise the liberal humanist subject: her superego is underdeveloped, her sense of justice flawed, and she has little autonomy. She is left, effectively, in a state of infantile dependency. She is more prone to illnesses that compromise any aspirant 'subjecthood' she may have; for example masochism (where she places herself as possessing multiple personalities). The very language of vagina/clitoris, Irigaray suggests, is informed by masculine parameters. In fact, women have a multiplicity of erogenous zones.[11]

Some contemporary French thinkers, for example Derrida and Foucault, are critical of psychoanalysis. Derrida is critical of it for positing – in sexual difference – the kind of opposition that is associated with logocentrism, a 'belligerent and murderous dichotomy' as Braidotti puts it,[12] as contrasted with a notion of difference which for Irigaray woman represents. Irigaray is, as we have seen, both critical of psychoanalysis and steeped in it. She emphasises the importance, if we are to 'speak as women', of reviving the pre-Oedipal phase, of symbolising the mother–daughter relationship, the period before subject/object boundaries are drawn up. Doing this (if it were possible) might reveal the underside of masculine, phallocentric discourse; it might undercut the emphasis placed on the notions of 'idea, subject, substance, transcendental subjectivity, absolute knowledge'.[13] It could involve valorising other metaphors than those of masculine *solidity*, for example, feminine *fluidity*. Fluids are sensitive to pressures. Fluids alter, in volume and force, according to the degree of heat under which they are placed. Fluids flow; they are continuous, compressible, dilatable.

Irigaray attempts to speak without presupposing the continuous 'I'. 'I am not; I *am* not; I am not *one*.'[14] She resists the definition: 'I *am* a woman.'

In her piece on Descartes, in the centre of *Speculum*, Irigaray throws doubt on Descartes' Cogito. She says: 'what if illusion were constitutive of thinking? What if I thought only after the other had been inserted, introjected, into me? Either as thought or . . .' (pp. 182–183). She suggests that the claim 'I am now thinking' is not self-verifying because I cannot be sure that it is indeed *I* that is doing the thinking. Descartes, according to Irigaray, can only claim that the move from 'I think' to 'I exist' is incorrigible if he assumes that his thought is non-illusory: that it is *he* who exists, and not, for example, someone else, 'the other', incorporated, introjected into his mind. Might it not be, as Irigaray mischievously suggests, the 'mother' who has been introjected?

Irigaray's point is that it is an assumption on Descartes' part that his thought processes are veridical; that his thought gives him a window onto his existence.

Furthermore, Descartes begins his enquiry with his own doubts and hesitations. He starts by assuming – himself – who doubts, thinks, etc. But how is this justified? To quote Irigaray once more: 'Descartes took good care not to suppose, not to presuppose that some other "I" might be doubting too.'[15] The Other, Irigaray points out, is restricted, in the first stage of Descartes' argument, to God, to 'he who might not take devilish pleasure in making him doubt everything'.[16] On what grounds does Descartes assume this privileged access to his own doubts as compared with those of other people?

But it is this presupposition, also, on Descartes' part, which leads him to conclude that, in the end, his perceptual processes do not deceive him about the existence of the external world. Irigaray says: 'But now, by a stroke of almost incredible boldness, it is the singular subject who is charged with giving birth to the universe all over again.' In this case, it is God who works like the mirror that ensures that what he sees represents what is there. God now guarantees the veridicality of his perceptual processes. But why should God do this? Irigaray once more: 'I think therefore God is: an infinite being who at every moment gives a new impetus to the formation of my subjectivity and what is more confers upon my words the truth of the objective realities that they aim for in ideas.'[17]

Throughout her writings, then, in different ways, Irigaray challenges the unitary, continuous self. In the present 'patriarchal' symbolic, she argues woman is constructed as 'other'; she is denied subjecthood.

Irigaray appears to be engaging in a similar project to many contemporary French thinkers in her challenge to the unitary character of the male subject. For her, though, this challenge is a feminist project: unlike Derrida, for example, who also valorises the non-unified female self and advocates the 'becoming woman' of philosophy, she aligns herself with feminist struggles against the multifarious forms of 'phallocentrism'.

One tradition of thought that apparently lies outside the terrain not just of Irigaray's thought but of French philosophy more generally, is contemporary liberal humanist analytical philosophy. I will argue, however, that there are striking similarities between the two traditions.

Contemporary Analytical Philosophy and the Self

Contemporary analytical philosophers, drawing on a tradition that begins in the seventeenth century with Locke and Hume, have sought to locate the criteria on the basis of which we identify a person as 'the same' over time. In the seventeenth century, Hume searched in vain for 'that which I call myself'. Following from the work of Locke and Hume, contemporary analytical philosophers have looked into three main areas in an attempt to locate criteria for the continuity of personal identity: spatio-temporal continuity, identity of brain and identity of some mental characteristic. On the first criterion, what makes a person one and the same over time is 'spatio-temporal physical continuity'.[18] Derek Parfit describes this as the 'standard view' in relation to physical objects. He gives two examples where spatio-temporal physical continuity means something different in each case, but appears to work as a criterion: the Pyramids and the moon. The first are static whilst the second moves in a regular way. In other cases, this criterion does not work: for example, a Camberwell beauty is first an egg, then a caterpillar, then a chrysalis, then a butterfly.

The above case illustrates the central problem with the theory: how rapidly can any possible alterations be made and, more strongly, how extensive can they be? In one of Roald Dahl's short stories, a 'person' survives as nothing but an eye attached to a brain. Dahl certainly assumes this character to be the same person as previously, since 'he' is taunted by his wife who blows cigarette smoke into his eye and watches the eye express fury. (The husband, in his previous embodiment, had hated this habit of hers.) Perhaps we have less difficulty with this kind of science fiction fantasy than we would were we to suppose a completely new body built around the original brain and eye. Would this be the same person or not? One philosopher, McGinn, is quite adamant that 'a person may have the same body as you but not be identical with you.'[19]

The difficulty, of course, with these kinds of thought experiment is that we have to rely on intuitions of 'sameness' in order to pronounce in these cases. If we were to compare this kind of example with the table beloved of other analytical philosophers, and ask ourselves, would a table that contained nothing except the 'form' of the original – a skeletal outline of its shape perhaps – and a small part of one of the legs, but which was different in every other respect, still be the same table? The answer, I think, would be 'no'.

The analogy, however, is not a very good one, and it illustrates, indeed, a further difficulty with the physical continuity criterion for personal continuity. Purely physical criteria do not differentiate *human* beings from tables, chairs and other physical objects. Human beings are thought to possess self-consciousness, and *physical* criteria do not appear to be sufficient to explain the continuity of a person *qua* person.

For this reason, some analytical philosophers have argued that it is identity of brain that is the major criterion for self-identity. What I really am is my brain. I am essentially my brain (see McGinn, p. 115 and Parfit, p. 273). The brain, it is said, is the location of the mind and of consciousness; it is the brain that is responsible for all key aspects of a person's functioning. It is, indeed, the activity of the brain that distinguishes Mary as the person that she is. As Parfit puts it, once again, 'The criterion of my identity over time – or what this identity involves – is the physical continuity, over time, of my brain and body' (Parfit, p. 204).

However, there is a common argument that is brought against this.[20] Since both hemispheres of the brain can function independently, it is logically possible for the two halves of a particular brain to be transplanted into two separate bodies and for each body to function. 'Identity of brain' theorists have maintained that if a brain were removed from one body and transplanted into a second, the person (who is identical with her brain) would remain. In the present case, however, the brain is transferred to two bodies, thus violating the principle that no one thing can be in two places at the same time. Pat Fitzgerald has extended this argument.[21] In response to the point that the two resulting people would not actually be the same,[22] in the qualitative sense, since one possesses the left hemisphere and the other the right, she argues as follows.

Imagine, for example, two empty, cloned-and-therefore-identical bodies awaiting transplant: Beatrice is to receive the left hemisphere of my brain, and Clarissa the right. Having received their brain portion, there would be no 'logical grounds' on which to claim that they were the same physical object. However, if we believe that what constitutes personal identity is to do with the brain, then we should believe that my personal identity has been transplanted. But the scenario seems to offer no logically coherent way of deciding which one of Beatrice or Clarissa would *be* me.[23]

The problem remains, then, if a one-to-two transplant is acceptable, on what grounds can both of the recipients not be said to be identified with the original person, so that that person is now in two places at once?

Another possibility, then, is to look to psychological criteria for our identity. The possession of some mental quality – self-consciousness or a soul – is said to differentiate *human* beings from animals. It is argued, then, that the identity of some mental characteristic or characteristics is what makes a person the same over time. The most commonly discussed characteristic is memory because it is memory that makes most people aware of their own continued existence over time. If a complete set of memories, therefore, were 'transplanted' from one person to another, then, on this criterion, the second person becomes identical with the first. One difficulty here is amnesia: if all memories are irrevocably lost and unamenable to recall, then it appears that that person (on the criterion) has ceased to be (see McGinn, p. 110). Additionally, one might hypothesise one-to-two (or more) memory transplants, thus violating, once more, the logical principle that one thing cannot be in more than one place at the same time.

There seems to be an intuitive problem, anyway, with the idea that (B) might wake up one morning with all my memories but no others of my characteristics, and I retain everything but my memories. Imagine that I retained my desire to swim each day, my existing interests (based on different memories but the same interests, nonetheless), my emotional characteristics, mental abilities and physical characteristics. Isn't it intuitively odd to claim that (B) is me and I am someone else?

When analytical philosophers have attempted to answer the question 'in what does the identity of a person consist?', they have found it very difficult to come up with an answer. Derek Parfit, in *Reasons and Persons*, argues that what matters – in the light of these arguments – is survival not identity. He contrasts a 'simple teletransportation' case with a 'branch line' case.[24] In the former example, Parfit on Earth becomes unconscious. A scanner destroys his brain and body while recording the exact states of all his cells. Parfit's blueprint is beamed to Mars where another machine makes a replica. Parfit then adds to his case the assumption that there is an overlap between the two identities: he supposes that Parfit on Earth remains conscious. He then discovers that a replica has been created but that he, Parfit, has been irreparably damaged and will die. Parfit claims that, in this case, although the person on Mars is not the same person as the person on Earth, he, Parfit has survived. Psychological continuity and connectedness, he suggests, is what counts, rather than identity. In the future, instead of saying that he, Parfit, will be dead, he will say: 'there will be no future experiences that will be related, in certain ways, to those present experiences' (p. 281).

Similarities between the Two Traditions

Irigaray, and other French philosophers who question the identity of the subject, are in the unlikely company of Parfit, who questions the notion of personal *identity* altogether. There are, of course, many and substantial differences between Irigaray and Parfit. For one thing, Irigaray's project is a feminist one, whilst Parfit's is not. Another difference is that it is difficult to see how one can ascribe agency to a 'subject' that 'is neither one nor two'. There is no one thing for Irigaray, therefore, about which one could either affirm or deny: she is the same person as she was. Parfit's survival concept does not have this consequence.

The similarities between Irigaray, the French thinkers and the analytical philosophers, however, run deeper than any I have so far mentioned.

Much of Irigaray's critique of the 'patriarchal symbolic' seems to assume that this symbolic is a liberal humanist one. This is suggested by her reference to notions of ownership, and by the central role that Descartes' Cogito occupies in *Speculum*.

Other contemporary French writers, too, who have spoken of the death of the subject, of a crisis of rationality, or of the overturning of the subject of consciousness, in fact use the (Cartesian) Cogito or the liberal humanist individual as their primary target. For Foucault, it is the (Cartesian) Cogito which is, in Rosi Braidotti's words: 'the keystone of the complex architectonics of classical rationalism'.[25] It is the Cogito that splits reason and its 'others' – madness, dreams, errors, the senses. Reason is affirmed over and against unreason. It is the Cogito and its reasoning powers which provide the foundation for the discourse of the human sciences, which 'objectify' 'the subject'. In the post-classical period, the Cartesian subject is replaced by the liberal humanist 'individual'. Foucault would like to reinstate madness, both as discourse in its own right, and as the foundation for reason.

For Deleuze, too, Descartes' Cogito is pivotal to classical rationality and to the form of subjectivity that has been the keystone of the powerful institutional role philosophy has occupied. Deleuze looks back to Spinoza, as against Descartes, for the origins of his world of 'desiring machines'. The analytical philosophers, too, in their attempt to characterise the identity of 'personhood', effectively take the view that the person is a liberal humanist individual.

But humanism – the belief in the power of human agency in history – as I pointed out in Chapter 1, neither began with liberal humanism, on the one hand, or with Descartes, on the other, nor is it co-extensive with either of these notions today. Neither the Renaissance humanist notion of the free and sovereign artificer nor the much later phenomenological and existential humanism 'constructs' women as objects of exchange, in the way that Irigaray suggests, nor does either equate the subject with self-consciousness in the way that many of the above writers assume of *all* humanisms.

There is another tradition of thought, then, including the work of Hegel, Marx and Sartre, that is humanist and quite different both from Cartesianism and from liberal humanism. For Hegel and Marx, for example, human beings are part of reality and produced by it. 'Man' is a rational being, according to Hegel, because civilisation itself is rational. The later Sartre, in *Critique of Dialectical Reason*, argues that individuals are both subjects and objects of history.[26] Heidegger too refused primacy to the human subject and the subject/object dualism that characterises Cartesianism and much liberal humanist thought. According to him, every individual is in-the-world.

None of these thinkers gives to 'the subject' the role that is presupposed by either Irigaray, and other contemporary French thinkers, or by recent analytical philosophers' attempts to define self-identity. All of the former group are critical of a system of thought where 'subject' is set against an externally existing object. In the systems their critique presupposes, subject is separated from object and 'man' stands outside the reality that is 'given' in consciousness. (There is also an idealist version, where objects exist only in so far as they are reflected upon by consciousness.) It then becomes important for the analytical philosophers who believe in this 'person' to ascribe an identity to it. The French critics of it, on the other hand, set out to deconstruct it.

In a picture, by contrast, where subject and object are seen to be inter-related, where the world is what it is as a result of its being lived in and worked on by humanity, the need either to define identifying characteristics or to deconstruct the 'rationalist subject' becomes less significant. It is less important to think about defining a 'subject' when that subject is part of the world, and a subject that is part of the world is not open to the deconstructive criticism of the French critics of the rationalist self. Indeed, not only is it less important, but it is likely to be impossible to offer an 'essential' definition of a subject that is an historical product, and knowledge of which is historical and relative. For such a subject, there is no 'outside' from which a transcendent self can contemplate 'the world' and its relation to it. There is no transcendent self that shares key features with every other such self. It is not surprising, on this viewpoint therefore, that the analytical philosophers were unable to find a definitive criterion for subject identity, since most such criteria – brain identity, identity of consciousness, identity of desires – presuppose an attenuated 'transcendent' self that is unlikely to describe key features of real historical persons. Furthermore, once the historical, in-the-worldly character of subjects is recognised, it is much less likely that 'the subject' will be seen to be masculine. Indeed, 'the subject' will have a variety of characteristics, depending on historical location, and there is no particular reason for any of them to be seen to be particularly associated with one or the other sex.

Having said this, however, there is a tendency for a theory that recognises the 'in-the-worldly' character of the subject to degenerate either into an idealism (where 'the world' is the product of thought) or a 'materialist' perspective where the world is seen to be independent of thoughts. Where this happens, there might develop an interest in defining the characteristics of the subject, and/or an implicit association of 'subjecthood' with masculinity. In fact, one can see the first of these two tendencies at work in the case of the analytical philosophers. Strictly, these philosophers recognise the 'in-the-worldly' character of the subject, for they do not assume subjects to be transcendent consciousnesses. On the contrary, they assume them to be living beings with a continuing identity. It follows from this recognition, however, that human beings are historical beings, both working on the world and being affected by it. It is likely, therefore, to be impossible to provide a transcendent definition of their essence. Yet these analytical philosophers implicitly move back into the realm of the transcendent self, as we have seen, in looking for this transcendent characterisation. Similarly, Irigaray and the other French philosophers implicitly associate the subject that is to be deconstructed with a transcendental other-worldly self.

With this chapter, I conclude the 'critical' section of the book, and I shall move on, in the chapters following, to describe, more positively, my own position.

5
Feminist Epistemological Communities

In Chapter 3 I defended a realist approach to meaning. This chapter begins my attempt to provide an alternative to postmodern feminism.

Traditionally, there are four issues in which philosophers with a predilection for epistemology have been interested. One is the question to which Socrates demanded an answer: 'What is knowledge?' What do we mean by 'knowledge'? Answers have ranged from Plato's, in *The Meno*, that knowledge is recollection, through to the theory to which analytical philosophers devoted so much attention, that knowledge is justified, true belief. Connected to the first question has been a second: 'Are we justified in claiming to know anything at all?' Descartes, the arch bourgeois individualist, during a break from the Thirty Years War in France in the seventeenth century, sat in his room, contemplating the extent to which he could trust his senses. Thought seemed to him to be far more trustworthy. Locke, a little later, argued just the opposite: that one could tell, by the nature or character of the perceptions, which ones were caused by qualities in objects and which arose out of the mind's own musings. Both thinkers, however, were 'foundationalists' to the extent of setting out to build the whole edifice of knowledge on secure foundations: in the one case 'thoughts' and, in the other, 'sensory experience'. Subsequent attempts to answer the questions, by those who regarded each of these solutions as inadequate, have been many and varied. They range from Kant's: 'No experience would be possible unless I had knowledge of the external world; I do have experience. Therefore I have knowledge of the external world'; through to pragmatist and 'common sense' solutions.

There have been two further questions to which epistemologists have sought solutions. One is a question often described, by twentieth century analytical philosophers critical of their seventeenth century predecessors, as 'psychological' – the question: 'Where does knowledge come from?

How does it come about?' The other is the question of validity: 'How are claims to know – beliefs or theories – validated?'

Recently, Sandra Harding has argued that feminist concerns are different from those of traditional epistemologists.[1] Feminist epistemologists are less interested, according to her, in the above questions, than they are in questions like: 'Why have "politically biased" research projects produced less partial results than supposedly "value-free" projects?' I would like to argue, in this chapter, that feminist epistemology can have something to say about questions three and four above.

This century, there have been three main theories about the origins of knowledge and about its validation. Broadly, these three theories could be described as empiricism, materialism and 'arguments from logical form'.

Each of these theories shares the following presupposition: knowledge is a matter for individuals, usually disembodied individuals, operating independently of their social and cultural contexts. It is this claim, above all, that has been challenged by feminist epistemologists. Feminist epistemologists have argued that knowledges are situated: that it matters who the knower is and where he or she is located. I would like to argue in favour of a situated view of knowledge that has some realist features and some 'perspectivist' presuppositions.

There are compelling reasons for upholding both of these, apparently incompatible, viewpoints. Sympathy for a 'realist' outlook arises from the conviction that sexism, class and racial injustice are not merely 'in the minds' of those experiencing the phenomena. Affinity with relativism, on the other hand, appears to follow from the recognition that, as individual subjects of knowledge, we construct pictures of reality that are structured by our own interests and values and by our social and historical locations. According to the realist, knowledge claims are true of reality, and the interests, the sex, the race of the knower do not affect that truth. The relativist, however, doubts that there are any such truths. All 'truth' is affected by the 'perspective' of the knower.

I would like to argue further that the appropriate epistemological subjects are communities.

Aristotelian 'Polis' and the Epistemic Community

I will draw on a tradition whose roots lie in the philosophy of Plato and Aristotle. According to Plato in the *Gorgias*, it is a precondition for engaging in rational enquiry that one should already possess and recognise certain moral virtues. A prior commitment to these virtues is required if enquiry is to proceed. In its Aristotelian dress, the knower is transformed in the process of gaining knowledge in the way that a craft worker is changed as he gains understanding and skill in the practice of his craft. Aristotle described the coming to terms with the discipline of philosophy itself on the model of a craft. The apprentice in the craft tradition has to learn not only what to do, in certain situations, but also how to iden- tify mistakes he or she may make in applying acknowledged standards – those seen to be the best available in the history of the particular craft.

Alasdair MacIntyre has articulated this model of knowledge in his book: *Three Rival Versions of Moral Enquiry*. He describes it as a per- spective that undercuts a conception in the history of philosophy that is shared by the 'Encyclopaedist' (broadly realist foundationalist) and the 'Genealogist', who may be a postmodernist or a relativist. Both these groups, he points out, share a view of history as unified: the Encyclopaedist sees a 'unified history of progress' (the progress of reason) whilst the Genealogist sees 'a unified history of distorting and repressing function'.[2] The view deriving from Plato, in the *Gorgias*, and Aristotle, rejects both horns of the dilemma. For them, history is not unified. Rather, the condi- tions for rational enquiry are historical and contextual. As MacIntyre puts it: 'membership of a particular type of moral community, one from which fundamental dissent has been excluded, is a condition for genuinely rational enquiry and more especially for moral and theological enquiry.'[3]. The enquirer, in the *Gorgias*, has to learn how to turn him or herself into a particular type of person – she makes herself like an apprentice, who learns from her teacher. Knowledge of reality is gained from the perspective of a community of broadly like-minded people – an extended 'guild'.

Some notion of an epistemological community analogous to MacIntyre's community allows both for a realist perspective – there is a reality out there and some descriptions of that reality are *wrong* – and for the idea that the nature of that reality is contextual and historical. Reality is shaped and altered by communities of people. But, further, it brings a degree of subjectivity to the process of knowledge construction and validation. Some features of the subject of knowledge matter: this subject is not a featureless mind or a 'filler' for 'S' in 'S knows that P'. Rather, she is historically located, and a member of the community.

Epistemological Communities

The following is a sketch of some of the arguments that can be put for the view that epistemological agents are communities: knowledge construction and validation, in fact, are co-operative, constructive endeavours. Knowl- edge construction and validation are not isolated, individual activities, and the notion of the individual implicit in such models – the isolated, autonomous, 'abstract' individual, is anathema. Anne Seller has spoken vividly of being unable to make sense of her own experiences in isolation from others.[4] Co-operative, constructive, 'other related' individuals enable the bringing to light of experiences, beliefs, values, that isolation does not.

It may appear that there are some knowledge claims that are independent of others. The examples beloved of traditional philosophers may appear to fall into this category. The claim 'this cat is on the mat' appears not to require any others for its construction and validation. However, Lorraine Code's telling example of the woman who consistently upheld a claim like this, when all others testified to the contrary, does illustrate that others are implicated even in such claims.[5] Code shows how difficult, if not impossible, it is to uphold any knowledge claim in isolation. The psychological experiments where subjects continually testify *against* their experience – claiming to see a red light, for example, because all other subjects have made a similar claim, despite the fact that they believe they see a green light – make an analogous point. Both examples illustrate the role played by others in knowledge construction and validation.

A second argument in favour of the idea that the appropriate epistemological agents are communities, stems from a common view of the practice of some of the sciences (although it need not imply accepting either that the sciences provide the paradigm of knowledge or that they always offer us knowledge at all). In this view, what comes to be viewed as knowledge is constructed by individuals in interaction with one another. These individuals interact by proposing hypotheses, testing them, comparing them with reports of experiential data. Additionally, they subject 'data' and any background assumptions to critical scrutiny. This critical scrutiny can include examining the consistency of the hypotheses and investigating the implications of any background assumptions.

As Helen Longino has argued,[6] this subjection of beliefs and hypotheses to critical scrutiny is pivotal to preventing beliefs being accepted only on the dogmatic ground of their widespread currency or their longevity.

Thirdly, it has been argued that a solipsistic knower is implausible in the light of human biology.[7] Human biology presupposes that we are social beings, and therefore seems to suggest that we are social knowers.

So, for discourses to be capable of becoming knowledges, there must be some kind of context, like the one provided by MacIntyre's appropriation of the medieval guild (though possibly not by the practice of the guilds, which were often the repositories of power and corruption), in which evidence, methods and presuppositions can be subjected to critical scrutiny. There must, additionally, be standards – such as coherence, accuracy – against which beliefs, evidence and assumptions are evaluated. In addition to the 'logical' or methodological standards, communities might also include standards such as those adopted by the guilds – the standard of facilitating particular activities, like the understanding of logic or rhetoric or enabling the activity of book-binding. They might also include broader aims, for example, understanding particular types of social interaction.

Some members of communities might function as 'teachers' or authority-figures in relation to others, but only in so far as this status is conferred on them by virtue of greater experience in the domain. Thus, some members of a particular community will know more about book-binding or socialist feminism than others. These individuals will be in a position to facilitate the learning of others. This role, I would argue, is an important one in the growth and development of knowledge: without the greater understanding of my peers and my teachers, I could not possibly have come to the limited understanding I now have of feminism or of epistemology. Members of the communities, therefore, need not be cognitively equal. However, of course, the 'wisdom' of the teachers must not be allowed to degenerate into dogma. The views of the teacher must be subject to critical scrutiny.

I would like to argue that an additional feature of an epistemic community is the Aristotelian collective or joint commitment to certain ends or values. In the scientific case, as Thomas Kuhn has argued, communities of 'experts' share certain ends, assumptions and presuppositions.[8] The questioning of one of those assumptions may lead to the dismantling of the community. In other cases, values may be less clearly set out, and may require much reflection and discussion before they emerge. Examples of such communities might be feminists as a group, lesbian feminists as a group, black feminists or feminists against censorship. Each community shares a set of values in common – that sexism is wrong, that racist feminism is wrong and that censorship is to be condemned.

One of the questions, according to MacIntyre in *Whose Justice? Which Rationality?*, that Aristotle set himself was: how could the Greek 'polis' be justified over its rivals?[9] The 'polis' was the institution whose concern was not with this or that particular good 'but with human good as such, and not with desert and achievement'.[10] When human beings are fully rational, on the Aristotelian perspective, it is the good and the best which supplies them with the ultimate end or goal. For Aristotle, in the *Nichomachean Ethics*, the person who is separated from his social group is deprived of the possibility of justice, and indeed some of the key qualities of a human being. People are disciplined and educated by the justice of the polis.

Aristotle's view that one is educated, in the polis, in the art of practical reasoning, and in the various virtues, is helpful in the present context. The community of socialist feminists, for example, might function analogously to a Greek 'polis', in educating its members about sexism and its causes. This education will involve disciplining sexist desires and feelings, and training 'the character' for the life of a 'good' (non-sexist) person. For Aristotle, one cannot be practically rational without being virtuous, and vice versa: for our non-sexist community, training in practical rationality and in anti-sexism helps generate knowledge.

Some epistemic 'communities', indeed, – in both the scientific and non-scientific cases – may come together by the 'functional interconnecting of unintended consequences' (to use an expression from Habermas – he calls these 'system integrated communities'), rather than from consensus about norms, values or ends. Habermas himself uses the capitalist economic system as an example of the former, and the modern, nuclear family as an instance of the latter. I would not go so far as to suggest, with Habermas, that the distinction is one of kind, yet something like the notion of 'system integrated' communities is useful to describe the basis on which some communities might come together. Feminists as a group originally came together out of a hunch that there were experiences, beliefs and practices that they might share. Women in consciousness raising groups, for example, were not originally aware of the set of values that, latterly, they have come to share. It took participation in the group to bring these values to light. Once they did emerge, however, epistemic activity pertains to the consequences of upholding those values for any claim to knowledge that might come within the purview of the community. Some communities, then, will function epistemically, on the basis of a combination of shared views, ideas and 'system' induced ends of which some or all of the group participants may be unaware.

An epistemic community, I suggest, then, will be a group of individuals who share certain fundamental interests, values and beliefs in common, for example, that sexism is wrong, that racism is wrong, and who work on consequences of these presuppositions. These individuals are particularly interested in the truth of their views, and in providing evidence for their truth. Members of one epistemic community may additionally be members of diverse other social, cultural and political groupings. They may have arrived at their membership of a particular epistemic community by creative interaction, including 'productive' conversations.[11] Epistemic communities, just like real social groupings of people, will contain members who are unequal in respect of power and status, but these inequalities will stem from something other than the characteristic by virtue of which the grouping constitutes an epistemic community. Epistemic communities, then, will be 'imagined' communities in something like Anderson's sense.[12] Sometimes their members may not share any form of social interaction. They may never communicate with one another, even by E-Mail. They form a collectivity by virtue of the values that they share and through their collective interest in providing evidence for the truth of their views. Thus, feminists worldwide (and some might refuse the label, see Seller[13]), despite our numerous disagreements, share a commitment to modifying and helping to eliminate power differentials based on gender. Some feminists may disagree with that way of describing the above matter; feminists may argue about what 'gender' means and what 'power' means and how these differentials have come about. Yet there is a broad commitment to a set of values, and it is this commitment, I am suggesting, that makes feminists as a group, worldwide, an epistemic community.

Knowledge, Validation and Emancipatory Values

What do we do when two epistemic communities disagree about a particular claim or claims? Some might go so far as to say that racists and anti-racists don't just disagree; rather they operate from incommensurable frameworks. No aspect of the racist's viewpoint can be compared with that of the anti-racist, because the corresponding terms in each theory differ in meaning.

I have argued in Chapter 3 against such a view of meaning. I disagree with the viewpoint, therefore, that the same word has a completely different meaning in two communities.

We might not believe in this radical form of relativism or incommensurability, but still have two communities making conflicting claims about reality.

Some disagreements between communities may be resolved by adherence to logical principles, like the principle of non-contradiction. Take, for example, adherents to a set of presuppositions about matter and the phlogiston theory of combustion versus commitment to the oxygen theory. The former group assumed that a substance was expelled – phlogiston – from the burning entity. Substances, however, gained in weight after burning. Therefore, the community of scientists who advocated the phlogiston theory had to argue either that phlogiston had negative weight – a view which contradicted their assumptions about weight – or that the general law of the conservation of matter was not applicable to combustion. Rather than adopt either of these two strategies – which would have presupposed rejecting one of the fundamental presuppositions of the community – the solution for that community was to reject phlogiston.

A similar kind of case can be made about philosophers who have accepted certain views about human rights, but have excluded women from these rights. Once they recognise that it is not possible to exclude women from the domain of human beings, then either the view of rights must be rejected, or it must be made applicable to women. In this case, again, it is appeal to consistency which helps determine which claims are accepted or rejected.

An insight from Sandra Harding will enable us to add to this. In her latest book, in the chapter 'Strong Objectivity', Sandra Harding argues persuasively that 'objectivism' – dispassionate, value-free science – is just the mirror image of epistemological relativism.[14] Instead, she suggests, *true* objectivity requires both cultural relativism, and maximally liberatory social interests. 'Objectivism' operationalises objectivity both too narrowly and too broadly – it is too narrow in that its 'value-free' character perpetuates sexist, racist and other values. Its 'value-free' nature encourages a blindness about these values. But it is also too broad in that it requires the elimination of all social values and interests. However, she argues, not all values have the same bad effects on the results of research. *True* objectivity must involve the examination of *all* the possible causes of human beliefs, including the values of the believer. Strong objectivity, she argues, must extend the notion of scientific research to include powerful background beliefs. I would demur from the idea that it includes *all* beliefs, since some will be unconscious and it would anyway be impossible to know whether one had investigated all of them.

Extending Harding's point, we can say that the interests/values/beliefs of some communities will be less emancipatory or less egalitarian than others. This factor will contribute to determining which of the two perspectives is accepted as true. The Nazi or the Serbian nationalist, for example, excludes Jews and blacks in the former case, and Bosnian Muslims, in the latter, from the treatment generally regarded as being due to human beings. Their values commit them to denying certain people the rights and the attributes of humanity. Some underpinning values, then, will be more emancipatory than others.

Emancipatory Values and Knowledge (1)

I am using the concept 'emancipatory' in the following sense: a value will be emancipatory if it contributes to removing oppressive power relations. Emancipatory values are not absolute, nor is it possible to say exactly which values they are. Values will be emancipatory relative to others: so, for example, liberal values are emancipatory relative to Nazism because they help us understand anti-semitism, but not relative to feminism. It may be argued, however, that this claim is not uncontroversial. Gayatri Chakravorty Spivak, for example, has written of the difficulty of judging whether white liberal colonial values were emancipatory for Indian women even in the extreme case of their disallowing suttee – the burning on the funeral pyre.[15] I would urge us, however, against a relativism of value which induces us to accept that a system which calls for the death of its practitioners may be preferable to an 'enlightened' liberal colonial one. I would urge us to accept some limitations on our relativism and suggest that, as a minimum, a value is more emancipatory than another if it has the effect of removing a person or a group of people from subjugation. At its most extreme, policies which subjugate would be those, like suttee and Nazism (although I am not, for a moment, failing to recognise the enormous disparities between these two cases), which lead to the death of the subjugated grouping. A less extreme case would be policies, like those of the South African government until very recently, and many liberal democracies early this century, which denied people fundamental rights – an obvious example would be the right to vote. I believe that it would be very difficult, except in the case of a grouping who were likely through perversity or irrationality to vote in a government that denied them even more fundamental rights, to defend the view that denying a group the right to vote was actually more emancipatory than offering them that right. The question arises, of course, emancipatory for whom? Offering the vote to black people in South Africa, it may be said, is emancipatory for them but not for whites in South Africa; giving the women the vote in the UK early this century was emancipatory for them but not for men. I do not wish to press the case – though I think that one could – that denying a particular grouping the vote actually has an adverse effect on the subjugator, as some have argued that racism adversely affects the racist. Nor do I want to argue, in classical liberal vein, that there are certain rights that ought to be open to all. I am suggesting, rather, that a set of values that upholds a particular right for a wider range of people, is more emancipatory than a set of values which does not do this.

I have given two examples of emancipatory values. One could imagine a scale of types of emancipatory value, ranging from values that prevent the killing of a particular grouping versus those that do not, through values that advocate the extending of fundamental rights to a wider range of people, and on to less 'extreme' cases. Such cases might include values that helped prevent unconscious or institutional discrimination against particular groups. Broadly, though, all emancipatory values help remove some group from subjugation. A value will be more emancipatory than another if it helps remove more people from subjugation, or helps clarify a greater number of types of subjugation – for example subjugation of women in general and lesbian women.

Emancipatory Values and Knowledge (2)

How, however, can this commitment to emancipatory values lead to knowledge? One kind of argument stems from feminist standpoint theory, but its logic, I believe, leads away from this outlook. Sandra Harding has argued persuasively that taking the standpoint of 'women's lives' has contributed to the growth of knowledge.[16] The agenda of the sciences, she argues, has been created as part of a racist, bourgeois, heterosexist and imperialist project. The 'knowledges' produced are therefore partial. The standpoint of 'women's lives', she suggests, adds a dimension that is hidden from the viewpoint of the abstract individualist, liberal stance. In biology, the standpoint of women's lives has revealed that women as well as men have evolved.[17] Woman the Gatherer played as significant a role as man the Hunter in the origin of the species. In another domain, starting from the standpoint of women's lives has revealed women's moral development to be something other than immature or deviant (as many male philosophers, historically, have viewed it).[18] Feminist researchers have shown how sexist and androcentric bias in all the sciences have affected the results of research, the methods deployed, the problems selected for investigation and the hypotheses generated.

Harding's argument is multifaceted: it is first that adding to the numbers of research scientists in itself has good effects on the results of scientific research. Excluding women, African men and other groups cannot, she suggests, benefit the results of scientific thinking. Additionally, she argues that the metaphors often deployed in science, for example, the metaphor of nature as female or of nature as a machine are not incidental to the research programme, but pervade the culture of any given scientific community, and blind its adherents to the fact that they are just that: metaphors. Thirdly, she argues that political struggles influence scientific knowledge. For instance, they brought modern science into being. 'The new physics advanced precisely because it both expressed the ethos of an emerging class (materialism, anti-elitism, progress) and also provided the means for expressing that ethos in technologies that could materially advance that class.'[19] Similarly, feminist struggles have influenced the agendas and results of the sciences.

I think it is important to untangle a number of different strands in Harding's text. It is also important that we make precise just what can be demonstrated from the kinds of argument Harding offers. First of all, although Harding has a legitimate point in her claim that excluding representatives of certain groups cannot help the advancement of knowledge, the converse – that allowing representation to all, on grounds of democracy – leads back to the kind of relativism that Harding wishes to reject. There must be some way of distinguishing between viewpoints, in order to describe one as less false than the other. Harding argues that adding to the numbers of research scientists in itself has good effects on the results of the research. If the extra scientists, be ·they lesbian women or African men or any other under-represented group, are either ineffective in the research area, or wholly in tune with dominant cultural values, their mere presence will have no positive effects on the development of knowledge. If, however, they are both effective and committed (explicitly or implicitly) to values that are, relative to others, more emancipatory, then they could help further the progress of knowledge. Harding's central argument: that the model for good science should be guided by liberatory social goals and interests, is close to the position I would like to advocate. A commitment to these goals can reveal gaps, discontinuities, partialities in knowledge. An example of this is the way in which a commitment to the perspective of lesbian women can reveal the implicit heterosexism in some feminists' thought. This is an advancement of knowledge – an opening up of horizons for all. Another is that thinking from the perspective of African lives can reveal aspects of the commonly accepted (in western circles) story of the 'origins of modern science' as Eurocentric and partial. I would distinguish my view from Harding's, however, and argue that it is not the experiences of any particular group that reveal the gaps and particularities in any viewpoint, but rather it is, in a significant way, the emancipatory values from which the group speaks. In each of the above cases, I would argue that it is the commitment to these values that is key. It was not lesbians as a group who revealed the heterosexism and hence the partiality of, for example, Freud's thought, rather it was those lesbians committed to undermining institutional hetero-sexism, in other words, those lesbians committed to the emancipation of lesbians from heterosexism. (Of course, those who revealed the gaps had to be committed to more than this: they also had to have an interest in Freudian theory.) Without that 'consciousness' on the part of some lesbians, other lesbians might have remained equally blind to aspects of institutional heterosexism. Again, it was not 'the perspective of African lives' that revealed the Eurocentrism of the story of the origins of modern science. Rather it was, again, the emancipatory values of those African people who have been committed to undermining institutional racism (and who, again, had the interest in the area). I would demur, therefore, from the view that feminist women speak for all women, that anti-heterosexist lesbians speak on behalf of all lesbians and that anti-racist African people speak for all African people. In a sense, of course, they do, because they are revealing gaps in knowledge that will benefit the whole of each group. Yet they may, on the other hand, be revealing matters that would not speak on behalf of the lesbian, for example, who is fundamentally convinced of the non-existence of institutional heterosexism.

Some white, privileged men have furthered the development of knowl-edge because they have been explicitly or implicitly committed to liber-atory values. The white, male scientists who contributed to the scientific revolution and the growth of modern science were committed to the liberal 'equal rights for all' values which were liberatory for many at the time.

In other words, it is not the identity of the group members of, for example, African people that revealed the Eurocentrism of modern science, it was rather those African people who spoke from a commitment to the emancipation of Africans from white domination. One does not have to be African to hold these values; potentially, anyone would be able to join the relevant community. Part of the answer to the question 'how did a commitment to emancipatory values lead to the advancement of knowl-edge?' then, is that these values often enable the bringing to light of infor-mation which is hidden from view. Repressive values can blinker the vision of the knower.

I would like to elaborate on the differences between my position, and that of Harding, by looking at some of the arguments against standpoint theory. Some of these have been well documented. I would like, however, to rehearse some of them, in order to bring to light the differences between the respective positions of Harding and myself.

Criticisms of Standpoint Theory

Harding advocates taking up the standpoint of 'women'. But early critics of standpoint theory, for example Jane Flax, argued, however, in postmodern vein, that there cannot be a *single* way that 'patriarchy' has permeated thinking. She finds problematic the idea of '*a* feminist standpoint which is more true than previous (male) ones'.[20] 'None of us can speak for women because no such person exists except within a specific set of (already gendered) relations.'[21]

For her, 'feminist theory' 'is a type of postmodern philosophy'.[22] I would concur with Flax that there is no one woman's standpoint. I disagree with her, however, in her claim that there is no feminist standpoint that is more true than previous male ones. On the contrary, whilst it is certainly the case that there is a multiplicity of standpoints, values, outlooks amongst feminists, there is a shared set of values that make feminists feminist. There is a collective commitment to the undermining of oppressive gender-based power relations. To deny that, is, as I have argued earlier, to undermine feminism altogether. This is very different, however, from the position I understand to be Harding's standpoint theory, which is that women have a shared perspective by virtue of their being women. I believe that there is no such shared outlook.

Another kind of difficulty with feminist standpoint theories has been articulated by Harding herself. She points out that some observers of African and Afro-American social thought have posited an African world view which, they imply, could be the origin of a successor science and epistemology. As Harding puts it: 'What they call an African world view is suspiciously similar to what in the feminist literature is identified as a distinctively feminine world view.'[23] These theorists argue that, for example, the 'rational economic man' of neoclassical economic theory is, in fact, *only* European. One writer, Vernon Dixon (quoted in Harding), locates the key difference between the two world views in the ' "man to object" v. the African "man to person" perception of the relationship between the "I" or self (Man) and everything which differs from the I or the self.'[24] In the Africanised world view, as in the 'feminist standpoint' world, there is no gap between the self and the phenomenal world.[25]

These African studies suggest that there may be a multiplicity of 'standpoints' – Caribbean, Asian, Cypriot, lesbian and more – from each of whose perspectives, the 'Enlightenment' world is the world of the dominant other. It renders doubtful once again, therefore, the idea of a specifically *women's* epistemological standpoint. What it suggests is that there may be certain epistemological features shared by any 'standpoint' that emerges from a collectivity that traditionally has stood in the position of 'dominant other' in relation to an oppressor.

Even this perspective, however, is rendered questionable by a third type of criticism of feminist standpoint theory. According to this criticism – articulated by, amongst others, Jean Grimshaw – there are plenty of white male 'oppressors' in the history of philosophy who have put forward philosophical views that stand in opposition to the Enlightenment human- ists.[26] The criticism runs thus: with regard to almost any position that has been described by feminists as a 'masculine' viewpoint, there are priv- ileged white male philosophers who have criticised it. Therefore, it is very difficult to speak of a 'women's' epistemological stance. 'Masculine' types of philosophy are multiple and varied.

Harding, herself, has advocated commitment on the one hand to the 'women's standpoint' and, on the other, to the standpoint of 'the lesbian', 'the African' and any group that is marginal or 'other' to the lives of the dominant group in any culture, period or establishment. She says: 'There is no single, ideal woman's life from which standpoint theorists recom- mend that thought start. Instead, one must turn to all the lives that are marginalised in different ways by the operative systems of social stratifi- cation.'[27] But it is difficult to see how one can take up the standpoint of all women, since thinking from the perspective of lesbian lives might contradict the perspective of other women's lives. If, for example, Butler were taken to be right, then the concept of 'woman' as advocated by many who think from the outlook of women's lives is a heterosexist construct, and it is certainly not in lesbians' interests to think from its perspective. The outlook of African women may contradict that of the white, American, middle class woman. In a way, Harding acknowledges this point when she allows for the white man to take on the standpoint of the lesbian woman (and thereby learning a lot about himself and his culture as well as about African lesbian women) but it casts doubt on her notion of a specifically 'women's' standpoint.

My own position, however, does not have these consequences. Rather than suggesting that an epistemological stance follows from the identity of the group holding it, as Harding implies that it does, my own position allows for a multiplicity of individuals to come together, in an epistemic community, so long as the members of that community share certain values in common.

Harding points to the Hegelian master–slave metaphor and Lukácsian Marxism as the philosophical roots of her theory.[28] In Lukács' version of historical materialism, the 'knowing subject' is the proletariat. In history, for him, understood through his Hegelianised version of historical mate- rialism, this subject produces itself as object. The object of knowledge is an evolved one: it is the present or some aspect of the present, and knowl- edge of the past is seen as retrospective reconstruction of the steps that led up to the present. When the theory, historical materialism, has become identical with its object, criticism of the object becomes self-criticism. For Lukács, only the proletariat is capable of achieving the requisite self-consciousness, because it is the only class which has to destroy all the inhuman conditions of life under capitalism which led to partial visions of the world, in order to liberate itself.

Harding draws an analogy between the Lukácsian proletariat and marginal groupings in general – for example, women, African Americans, lesbian women. Additionally, according to her, men can take up the 'women's standpoint' and non-lesbians can take up that of the lesbian. However, it is difficult to see how she can both acknowledge the Lukácsian point that it is by virtue of your social position as a marginal individual that you gain a special perspective on the world and simultaneously suggest that anyone can take up that social position. On the Lukácsian view, relationship to the means of production defines your class position and thereby your epistemological perspective. It is because of the social class position you occupy that you have that epistemological advantage. Harding cuts the ground from under her feet by removing that connection between social position and epistemological outlook. Harding's argument is problematic in both ways: if she argues that it is because of their special relationship to reproduction that women can take up a particular standpoint, she is open to the objection that, in a complex society, there are multiple, potentially contradictory, relationships to reproduction and, additionally, there are other kinds of social relation that condition subjectivity. If, on the other hand, she argues that anyone can take up the 'women's' standpoint, then it is difficult to see what makes it specifically a *women's* standpoint.

But there are additional difficulties with revamped standpoint theory which were also problematic for Lukács. For Lukács, though not for Harding, 'truth' is equated with knowledge of the totality. This truth will come about when the working class – the 'universal' class for him – brings about socialism. But the trouble for him, is that the working class may not bring about socialism. The truth of the theory, then, is made to rest upon a possibility that may not become actual. And these are tenuous grounds upon which to rest the truth of a theory. Harding's standpoint theory does not have *this* consequence because she does not believe in this Hegelian form of universalism: she does not argue that the women's standpoint gives access to a 'truth' to which the dominant standpoint does not. However, her theory is open to the objection that the women's standpoint may *not* reveal gaps in the dominant one: women may, and often have, wholly imbibed the dominant view: they may rely on arguments from authority; they may be empiricists; their *experience*, something to which Harding attaches a lot of importance, might fit the dominant paradigm. Without some independent account of why the women's standpoint represents the *true* one, there is no guarantee that it will do so.

Instead of adopting the standpoint of 'the woman', I have been suggesting that we take up the standpoint of communities of individuals which are more committed to emancipatory values.

Epistemological Communities and Values

Postmodern feminists may, however, question my approach: they may argue that it is still too 'empiricist'. I am arguing that one viewpoint, that from a community committed to emancipatory values, gives greater access to knowledge than viewpoints from other types of community do. But that 'knowledge' is only so from a particular standpoint: the standpoint from lesbian emancipatory values might be oppressive to some further grouping, as liberal values were for the working class. Communities committed to emancipatory values do not so much reveal gaps, as present things in a new, enlightened way for some people at particular moments, but those viewpoints are equally oppressive for other groups.

In response to this, I would argue that communities of people, such as liberals in the nineteenth century, or feminists or lesbian feminists in the twentieth century, or black feminists, who are committed to the emancipation of that group from dominant power structures, can provide 'insights' into knowledge that were previously hidden from view. The communities of nineteenth century liberals (operating from liberal values) revealed the class and status-bound nature of claims that had previously been taken for granted; straight, white, feminists (operating from their particular emancipatory values) revealed that claims previously thought to be applicable universally, in fact related only to men, and the community of lesbian feminists has revealed similar insights about other feminists' claims. Each of these groups is committed to the emancipation of a particular group – humanity, women and lesbian women. In general, groupings which have an interest in emancipation have offered these kinds of 'radical insights' about the world. These insights, whilst they do not give us greater access to 'the truth', nor are they obviously 'less false' in some cumulative way, have nonetheless opened a window on the world which is revealing and which could be described as providing 'new knowledge' or 'new truths'. It is rational, I would suggest, for the viewpoints of the groupings providing access to radical insights, to be accepted over the views of their counterparts, since it is in this sort of way, so long as these viewpoints have been subjected to the process of critical scrutiny in a community, described earlier, that knowledge advances. In contrast to these groupings, those who, like some of those on the far right, seek to restrict rights to particular people, close down knowledges and introduce blinkers on perception.

It is important that too great a claim is not made for the power of emancipatory values in legitimating beliefs. It is not possible to claim that beliefs generated from a commitment to emancipatory values lead to knowledge *per se*. Rather, the claim must be that they are true for the moment, they are less distorted than their counterparts. In turn, the values themselves must be historicised: there is no set of values that is absolutely 'better' than any other set. I am not suggesting, then, that a commitment to emancipatory values gives one greater access to '*the* truth'. Rather, I am suggesting that the viewpoint of the community committed to emancipatory values provides 'radical' insights that can be called knowledge, because they enable one to see the world in new and enlightened ways.

The Ultimate Riposte

The postmodern feminist might question all of this, however. She might continue to maintain that the standpoint of the community committed to emancipatory values is just one more standpoint or perspective amongst many: it has no greater claim to epistemic validity than any other.

To this riposte, I would respond as follows. This hypothetical postmodern feminist is not far away from the ancient sceptic or the contemporary Sisyphean, who argues that life is absurd. This postmodern feminist claims, of any particular stance, that it is just one view among many, and there is no way of determining the validity of any one outlook over any other. But this is not far removed from the claim that it does not matter which beliefs we uphold or which actions we perform for what motives, since, in the end, they may be absurd. If it is not possible to distinguish one set of beliefs or form of activity from another, then it does not matter what we think, believe or do, and, ultimately, all beliefs and actions are absurd. Nagel has argued that even if human beings attempt to confer significance on their lives by seeking broad ultimate concerns, such as feminists have found in their political ventures, these concerns cannot confer significance on life unless they are themselves meaningful.[29] And, he suggests, we can step back from the purposes, justifications that any individual (or group) gives for any action or belief, and doubt their point, in just the way that the sceptic about knowledge questions belief in the existence of everyday objects. We can, he says, 'step back also from the progress of human history, or of science, or the success of a society, or the kingdom, power, and glory of God and put all these things into question in the same way.'[30]

I doubt, however, whether the self that doubts so much about its projects is a coherent self at all. I would strongly advocate distinguishing doubts about 'the progress of human history', which I would call 'rational doubts' for the reasons given earlier, from stepping back from *any* belief system. The postmodernist feminist is effectively doing that, in questioning the validity of the examples of 'knowledge progression' described earlier. Earlier sceptics' selves, for example Descartes' thinking thing, are not capable of being individuated or distinguished from other selves. Kant's noumenal self, too, is such an attenuated thing that it is difficult to suppose it to have any *identity* at all. Nagel's self and the postmodernist feminist self become like these. The self that steps outside all its projects or that questions whether any of them has value over any other, becomes an attenuated thing. The self that steps outside all its projects, and doubts their value, is one that has effectively left behind all that belongs to it as an embodied, affective, suffering creature. It has left behind its memory and its history, its ties and its relations to others. In fact it is rather like the Kantian, Rawlsian, Kohlbergian moral self that is like all other selves, and yet akin to none of them. I would question whether such a self has the capacity to doubt, since it has abandoned its will to find meaning in all possible projects to some fantasmal noumenal realm.

All who have argued that life is ultimately meaningless, or who have adopted this kind of postmodernist stance, have, I suggest, taken the standpoint of the 'generalised other'. Everyone, ultimately, is viewed as being like oneself. In so doing, all concrete differentiating qualities disappear. But if, as I have suggested, this conception of the self is ultimately incoherent, then this kind of stance on the meaning of life is also incoherent. As Susan Bordo says, of the postmodern body: (it is) 'no body at all'.[31]

In order to ask meaningful questions about the 'meaning of life', one has to adopt the stance of the concrete other.[32] In other words, one has to recognise differences amongst people: one has to see each person as an individual with a history, an identity and a will to pursue particular projects. One can, and indeed must, stand outside each project in order to compare it with others, to justify one as better than another. But this does not entail adopting the Nagelian stance, rather it involves the capacity to empathise with others, to understand their projects and the motives from which they are carried out. This certainly does not mean bracketing off these projects to some hypothetical noumenal realm from where they become indistinguishable from one another.

Taking, instead, the standpoint of the 'concrete' other, and in particular the epistemic community, gives one a basis upon which to distinguish between viewpoints.

Epistemic Community

Postmodern feminists may continue to argue, however, that this liberal approach to epistemology neglects a key feature of the knowledges that, in fact, come to be taken to be 'true': their links with power. Postmodern feminists argue not only that the positioning of knowing subjects is crucial in determining the acceptability of claims to know: but further that there is an integral connection between 'dominant' epistemologies or 'discursive-formations', 'dominant' intellectuals and power more generally. Some feminists (Gayatri Chakravorty Spivak might fall into this category) would link this power-knowledge complex to wider capitalist and imperialist social structures. Dominant power-knowledge complexes function, in other words, both to maintain the social and economic status quo, and to reproduce the 'object' position of those minority groups or groupings they tend to designate as 'other'. Spivak's work illustrates not only the denial of voice to the subaltern 'Indian' woman, in certain forms of colonial discourse, but the denial of her identity altogether.[33] Many feminist philosophers have examined the link between, for example, Enlightenment epistemologies and the capitalist and patriarchal systems they served both to represent and reproduce.

However, although some well known classical epistemologies no doubt did serve to support and uphold dominant systems of power, it is important to point to the oppositional role occupied, in their own times, by such 'dominant' intellectuals as Hegel and Marx (to name but two white men).

But this historical claim is less important than the argument that it is vital, for political reasons, that we unhook 'knowledges' from power. The question of which forms of knowledge have been accepted historically, in capitalist and imperialist social structures, must be distinguished from the question of which ones ought to have been or ought to be accepted as true. My argument has been that one criterion of acceptability is the emancipatory content of the values upheld by a particular community. The actual position in the social hierarchy of those individuals is no doubt important: it is likely, indeed, that those who are positioned as 'subaltern' in respect of dominant groups will be in a better position to articulate true emancipatory values (since those values are the ones most likely to have been excluded by previous 'dominant' systems of thought). I do not, for a moment, wish to suggest that this project of determining which values are truly emancipatory is, in any way, an easy one: the conflicts, for instance, articulated between 'blacks' and Jews in the USA (by bell hooks and others), those between upholders of green politics and political groups concerned to defend jobs, for instance testify that the decision as to which values to uphold as 'truly' emancipatory is by no means an easy one.

But I would argue, further, that some 'power' is benign, that throwing out all 'authority' is to throw out the baby with the bath water. There is a distinction between authority (as is the case, for example, with some fundamentalist religious groupings) that is imposed, either by coercion or by 'enforced persuasion' on a community, and the sort of authority which figures in the Aristotelian community I have been describing. In the latter case, authority and tradition are essential prerequisites in knowledge-construction and validation. Without tradition and authority, no one could begin the process of knowledge-construction or validation. The postmodernist influenced feminist outlaws all systems of power. My epistemologist does not.

Collectivities and Communities

'Epistemic communities' are not 'communities' in the sense in which the term has been used in the 'New Left' of the eighties. In this discourse, the term 'community' is used as an alternative model of a 'collectivity' from that of 'class' or 'party'. This concept of community is used to refer to a group of people including all those previously excluded from social representation – for example, 'women', 'black people', gays and lesbians. Sociologists have objected that this notion has tended to encompass only the representatives of the various groups and not the groups themselves. My notion of 'community', as I have said, however, is closer to Anderson's 'imagined community': it incorporates people who may share no physical, relational or cultural ties.[34] Its boundaries are constantly shifting, and it may go in and out of existence. Some of its members, however, like the members of the Greek 'polis', will relate to one another and learn from one another.

The outlook I have described, although quasi realist, does not assume the Enlightenment realist 'view from nowhere'. It does not assume a non-located, non-contextual, non-value-laden God's eye perspective from which 'the truth' is revealed. Rather, the epistemic community is historically located, its beliefs and its experiences are inflected by the values that it holds. However, the nature of the values upheld by any one community are such as to undermine claims to 'the truth' made by other communities. The claims of any one community are not true for all times and in all places; rather they are open to constant revision by other communities.

In a sense, then, both realism and relativism are vindicated. The realist's insight that claims are true, not just for me or for a particular group, is vindicated. But the claim of some realists to have provided a 'view from nowhere' that mirrors unmediated 'experience' or 'the world' is not. The relativist's insight that all knowledge is provisional and contextual, is also vindicated; but her claim that viewpoints are true only for herself or for her community, is not.

The feminist epistemologist, therefore, can offer a response to two of the traditional epistemologists' questions: how does knowledge come about? and how are claims to know validated?

6
Feminism and Morality

Men and Women as Ethical Subjects

The previous chapter outlined a 'modernist' view in epistemology. In this chapter, I propose to look at the ethical dimension.

Several male philosophers who have held widely divergent views about the nature of ethical principles, have been in agreement that the roles of men and women as ethical subjects are different. Some of these figures have been quite explicit about the matter; others have made claims which have this implication. Thus, Aristotle, Rousseau and Hegel quite clearly claim that women are incapable of male standards of morality. Rousseau advocated excluding women from citizenship on the grounds that their 'virtues' are more properly located in the home. Hegel equates 'female consciousness' with the life of the family, a primitive stage in relation to the life of civil society.[1] In his pre-critical writing, Kant offers a view very much like that of Rousseau. In his *Observations on the Feeling of the Beautiful and the Sublime*, Kant assigns the sublime to men and the beautiful to women and continues as follows:

> Nothing (for women) of duty, nothing of compulsion, nothing of obligation! Woman is intolerant of all commands and all morose constraint. They do something only because it pleases them, and the art consists in making only that pleases them which is good. I hardly believe that the fair sex is capable of principles, and hope by that not to offend, for these are also extremely rare in the male.

Women, according to Kant, excel in a kind of feeling characterised by 'beautiful understanding' that is destroyed by learning.[2] They are passive rather than active; women are made for a life of dependence on men.

Jean Grimshaw has pointed out that women for Kant in *Observations on the Feeling of the Beautiful and the Sublime* are given just those qualities which, in the *Groundwork of the Metaphysic of Morals* are said not to carry true moral worth – feeling, benevolent sensations, complacency, reliance on particular judgements – and are denied those which do: abstract reasoning, principle and universal rules.[3]

Gilligan and Kohlberg

A contemporary Kantian is Kohlberg. Kohlberg acknowledges his debt both to Kant in the moral domain and to Piaget in the realm of cognitive science. Kohlberg conducted experiments which appear to show girls to be morally less mature than boys. When children are presented with moral dilemmas, he argues, girls pay more attention than boys to the concrete and particular and are less ready to apply universal moral principles to particular cases. Gilligan, a feminist critic, responded that Kohlberg was only measuring a certain kind of moral development: the development of conceptions of justice and rights.[4] Boys performed better in the experiments, Gilligan argued, because they tended to employ this kind of morality. There is, however, she argues, another type of morality, an ethics of care and responsibility, in which girls are more developed than boys. Women's moral judgement, she suggests, is more contextual; women pay more attention to the particularities of a case in judging how to act. There is a distinct feminine disposition to empathise with the particular other, as opposed to the masculine disposition to abstract from the particularities of the person and the case. These feminine characteristics come about because of women's greater responsibility for parenting.

A feminist ethics, therefore, is an ethic of *sympathy* – women sympathise and empathise with the situation at hand, whilst men will universalise from the context and reason abstractly about justice and rights. Whereas liberal, rationalist feminists might go along with the Kohlbergian sympathisers in describing the moral development of the girls in question as backward, Gilligan sees the moral system itself that derives from Kant as being part of the problem. Liberal, rationalist feminists are therefore advocating a course which is both impossible – women taking on masculine, androcentric ethical values – and undesirable – it replicates the very problem it was designed to solve. Gilligan describes the traditional androcentric view of morality as insufficiently rich; as too narrow.

Kohlberg has responded to the initial Gilligan critique. He has argued that the differential performance of girls and boys in the tests reflects variations in education and job experience. Women, he has suggested, have tended to take on occupations and roles that little fit them for the kind of abstract universalist reasoning necessary for proper moral development. Moral maturity requires the kind of experience that is only gained from work outside the home. In other words, he is denying that the differential results of his experiments reflect fundamental variations in the natures or the moral capacities of men and women. He further accepts that the notions of care and responsiveness enlarge the moral domain, but he argues that the two conceptions of morality – the one concerned with justice and rights and the other with care and responsiveness – pertain to different spheres of activity. The morality of rights and justice is appropriate for the 'public' domain; whilst care and responsiveness are appropriate where one's special concerns are to family, friends or group members. These divergent moralities may not specifically pertain to the two sexes; rather they have to do with variations in role and activity. There are overtones here both of Plato – for whom genuine moral development took place in the state or the polis – and more particularly of Hegel, who suggested that the care orientation had to do with the personal and familial; whilst genuine moral development was only possible in the public domain. Antigone's loyalties are to kinship and friends, but, Hegel claims, these sympathies are less significant than the loyalties of the man, which are to state and nation.

As well as Kohlberg's response, there has been a feminist reaction to Gilligan. Feminists who are influenced by postmodernism to a greater degree than Gilligan have argued that her ethical model is open to the same charge of false generalisation which she levelled at Kohlberg. Gilligan does not say 'which women, under which specific, historical circumstances have spoken (with a different voice)'.[5] Gilligan, it is often said, is generalising a particular perspective on to women.

It has also been argued that Gilligan's argument – that it is because of their nurturing experience that women acquire their 'caring' ethical perspective – implies that there is a moral duty to confine women to their mothering role, as a way of guaranteeing the presence in society of these caring qualities.[6] Furthermore, the notion of separate female and male moral reasoning has itself come in for critical scrutiny. Virginia Held suggests that, in most contemporary western societies, there is such extensive contact between men and women that it is difficult to believe in separate masculine and feminine cultural spheres. Men and women interact in such a wide variety of ways that there seems to be no particular reason to prioritise the notion of motherhood: there is no reason why this particular type of interaction should influence all other types of human relationship. It can, indeed, be an oppressive relationship, and other forms of interaction may actually provide better models on which to base ethical theory.

In the light of these critical points, feminists who take their postmodernism further still have, as we have seen, stressed the importance of recognising differences, and this has extended to a questioning of the possibility of any transhistorical, culture independent norms. Indeed, some have gone so far as to question the possibility of norms at all (since *any* norm is 'transcendent' to a degree). Liberals relied on the common humanity that everyone is supposed to share, and this common humanity grounded their commitment to norms: justice, equality and autonomy. Feminists like Gilligan, postmodernists would argue, use norms illegitimately if they question the notion of a common humanity.

I should like, in the next section of the chapter, to offer a different kind of response to Kohlberg and Gilligan. I would like to query the notion of reason deployed by Kohlberg. I will suggest that it is possible, contrary to some of the above feminist critics, to make generalisations, and to make reference to norms.

A Reworked Concept of Reason

At the heart of the Gilligan–Kohlberg debate, feminists have claimed, are divergent views about the nature of the subject, and the essence of personhood. Many feminists have argued, as we have seen in earlier chapters, that the classical epistemological subject – the subject of eighteenth century science and knowledge, the subject of much contemporary epistemological theory – is disembodied and disembedded. This disembedded subject is the subject of liberal, rationalist morality. Liberal rationalists, they have argued, in making moral claims, abstract away all qualitative differentiating features of individual agents, and consider human beings as intrinsically alike – alike in respect of their mental natures or capacities. But this is linked, it has also been argued, with a perspective on the nature or the essence of a person as having to do with the possession of *reason*. Within the western tradition, at least from Aristotle to Kant, human beings have been differentiated from non-humans (usually other animals) by means of the possession of reason. This kind of claim has been deployed in a variety of contexts, to perform a number of different functions – to justify ill-treatment or the killing of animals, to allow abortion and the switching off of life support machines, and to deny 'human' rights to women, slaves and children, who have at various times been regarded as deficient in this capacity.

Feminists have drawn attention to and criticised the disembodied and disembedded subject: it has been argued, for example, that the standard liberal view of the subject as a sovereign person, without a social context, reflects aspects of masculine experience. Using Chodorow and object relations psychoanalytic theory, it has been argued that the masculine childhood experience produces subjects that are more autonomous, more independent of the context in which they are located than female subjects. One feminist, Benhabib, has claimed that liberal moral theory is actually, therefore, conflicting with its own recommendation that moral judgements are reversible and universalisable.[7] The theory, she argues, is built on a notion of the subject that is actually *incoherent*. One cannot, she argues, treat others as disembodied and disembedded and simultaneously view them as *persons*. The notion of a person, without social and personal circumstances, is incoherent. We cannot discriminate between situations unless we have some knowledge of the persons in them. A morality like Kant's, which invites us to 'universalise' on the basis of 'like' situations, cannot in practice be applied, because situations do not come 'like envelopes' in a way which invites clear comparison.

This critique is a powerful one in its way, but there are, I believe, two problems with it, and interestingly enough, they pull in opposing directions. On the one hand, it is still too strongly influenced by the second strand of liberal theory – its commitment to a particular conception of reason, as lying at the heart of 'personhood'. On the other hand, Benhabib, I believe, exaggerates the extent to which liberals deploy the disembodied, disembedded subject. I will discuss these two aspects in turn.

The notion of reason in question is, explicitly or implicitly, in much of the work of the tradition, deductive reasoning.[8] Kant, in particular, participatory as he was in Enlightenment rationalism, offers a clear example of this. The application of his moral principles proceeds by deductive reasoning. The classic example of the application of the principle of universalisability in the *Groundwork* consists in showing that breaking promises is *incoherent* – not that doing so would be to act in a fashion that is contrary to some moral ideal; rather that acting so is incoherent, in just the way that breaking a logical rule is incoherent. For Kant, to be autonomous is to be a purely rational being: a being who acts only on universal principles.

Kohlberg is like the Kantians in that he sees moral development as a form of cognitive development, and this is construed in terms of the progressive application of principles of abstract, deductive reasoning in the moral domain. Moral rationality, in other words, consists in deriving judgements from moral principles, by deductive means.

A limitation of this conception of reason can be illustrated by an example. One of the interviews described in Carol Gilligan's *In a Different Voice* was with two children: Jake and Amy. Both children were presented with a problem Kohlberg had employed in his research. It runs as follows: a man, Heinz, has a wife who is dying, but he cannot afford the drug she needs. Should he steal it to save his wife's life?

In his solution, Jake considers a number of principles concerning human interaction, and describes the issue as a 'sort of maths problem with humans': it requires a logical prioritising of the various principles.

Jake is employing the abstract, deductive conception of reason. He sees morality as being about devising appropriate principles, and deductively reasoning from these to a particular case. Additionally, he believes he has to prioritise these principles in a fashion that is analogous to the logical

ordering of mathematical concepts. In the latter case, one might prioritise principles in such a way that the principle of non-contradiction is the
most fundamental of all; the principle of identity might follow that, and
others might follow in descending order. In fact, as Kuhn and many others
have pointed out, there is no 'logical' process of ordering even for the
principles of logic and mathematics. The fundamental 'presuppositions'
of a mode of scientific enquiry may have been agreed without any justification at all, as was the case, for example, with work within Newtonian
science. The basic Newtonian laws were accepted by many scientists
operating within the paradigm without question, as being in no need of
justification.

The problems of deploying this kind of model in the case of morality
are twofold. First of all, individuals – like Jake – sometimes appear to
believe there *is* some rationale for the acceptance of fundamental principles in the scientific case, and that this kind of rationale should be carried
over to morality. So Jake sees the moral dilemma as involving some
'logical' ordering of moral principles. First of all, Jake is wrong, in fact,
in supposing that there is always some rationale in the scientific case. But
secondly, he is employing a model of reasoning – some notion of a logical
ordering of principles – that may be inappropriate in the case of morality.
It may be neither possible, nor desirable, to 'rank' principles; it may be
inappropriate to rule out apparently inconsistent principles – such as
'stealing is always wrong' and 'stealing is sometimes right' (although not
actually inconsistent ones), and it may be unhelpful to use a kind of
deduction to derive the individual case from the principle. Benhabib, I
believe, is over-reliant on this conception of reason in her critique of the
disembodied subject.

Jake is not, I think, a special case. Kant, the rationalist moral theorist
par excellence, is very like him. He writes as though moral principles were
like universal scientific laws, applied to abstract, qualitatively indistinguishable rational autonomous beings. Like the objectivist scientist in
Popper's world, who strips the world of differentiating features, and
uses the principle of falsifiability to knock out recalcitrant theories, so
the Kantian first strips people bare, and then uses the principle of
universability to knock out recalcitrant moral principles. No matter
whether these principles are ethically valuable; if they do not fit the rationalist principle then they must be damned. Kant, therefore, like Jake, sees
morality as a kind of maths problem: his view of reason limits it to the
weeding out of contradictions, and the prioritising of principles according
to their universalisability. John Rawls, the modern Kant, adopts a similar
strategy – the fundamental moral principles for him: the principle of
justice, the principle of liberty and the 'difference' principle, are ordered,
a priori, in a quasi 'scientific' fashion. They are accepted as ultimate claims
that anyone in the original position would choose, in analogous fashion

to the way a Newtonian might take on board the presuppositions of 'his' theory.

... And of Emotion

The other side of the coin of the Kantian/Kohlbergian over-reliance on the limited notion of reason is that it depends, also, on a partial picture of emotion. Gilligan, at least in her early writings, may be endorsing this limited model of emotion. A more appropriate model, I would like to argue, is one that integrates Gilligan's 'care' perspective with that of Kohlberg to a greater degree.

Many thinkers, historically, have differentiated reason from emotion. Probably the classic exponent of the view that emotion is separate from reason – the motivator of reason – is Hume. But many others have reinforced this separation of reason and emotion. The way has been open, therefore, for reason to be associated with masculinity and emotion with femininity. Some have urged a necessary connection between reason and masculinity, whilst others have argued that this association is a contingent result of the environment in which men and women historically have been placed.[9]

Miranda Fricker has argued that the theory that separates reason and emotion could be described as 'positivist'. The 'positivist' view of emotion reduces it merely to physiological sensations, 'pure experience' along the lines of empiricist 'sense-data'. For example, I could be said to be experiencing anger when my pulse races, my muscles tighten. Fricker argues, against this view, that emotions may be present without the physiological manifestations, and the manifestations, conversely, without the emotions. She suggests that, when sensation is bound up with an emotion, it is not until reason interprets the sensation, that the sensation is registered. Fricker further claims that emotions have to have objects: they have to be about something. In other words, emotions contain a belief about their objects. They depend upon the world, she argues, both for their existence and for their definition. Emotions, therefore, are constructed by rational thought processes; they are, furthermore, socially constructed, in so far as they involve shared concepts and means of expression.

I think that there is a type of emotion – unconscious emotion or desire – which is not linked to reason in quite the way Fricker argues. We may experience desires where the belief about the object is unclear or where we are self-deceived about the object. We may, further, both misdescribe the emotion and focus on its object wrongly as when, for example, we direct hatred of a parent onto ourselves in the form of a denial of self-worth. In these kinds of case, we may need or want to go through a process of reasoning, involving analysis (or psychoanalysis) of the possible objects and the possible causes of the emotion.

That said, I believe that Fricker has made an important point about emotion, and it is one which can be used to illustrate a further limitation of the Kohlberg model of moral reasoning. Jake, in the above example, excised feeling altogether from his consideration of the morality of the question of Heinz and his wife. Amy deployed emotion, but perhaps in too limited a way.

Part of what is wrong with Kohlbergian morality, therefore, are the conceptions of reason and of emotion deployed. Instead of the narrow deductive concept of reason, I would advocate for morality a richer notion of reason that involves emotion. This concept flows from Aristotle's 'moral virtues' to which I appealed in the previous chapter.

The 'richer' notion of reason, in Aristotle, is naturalistic: some description of human nature forms the basis on which motives for moral behaviour are built up, and on which moral activity is focused. In Aristotle's view, morality aims to bring to fulfilment those features of our 'personhood' which are present as potentialities. To act rationally, for Aristotle, is to choose to behave in ways that will bring about the realisation of one's nature. Rationality, therefore, is embedded within our bodily as well as our mental natures. Moral decisions, in Aristotle's view, are related, not to the first principles of syllogistic reasoning, as they are with Kohlberg, but to our basic human needs and desires. Morality, therefore, becomes being a certain kind of person and behaving in certain ways.

I believe that there is an important kernel of truth for feminists in this naturalistic view. Men and women have needs and desires which flow from their sexed natures. (I shall have more to say on the notion of 'male' and 'female' natures in the chapter following.) It may be that consideration should be given, for example, in the case of a particular moral dilemma, to needs arising from premenstrual tension in a woman. One's nature, I believe, then, will play some role in determining moral choices. It is, of course, a vast empirical question to determine what counts as this nature, and many postmodernist critics of radical and cultural feminisms have argued that they have mistakenly taken cultural and social features of some women to be natural to all. I believe, however, that the appropriate response to this is not to reject the notion of a 'natural' grounding to morality *tout court*, but to recognise that the specification of what is natural is a difficult task.

I would urge, however, along the lines of the previous chapter, that a further important dimension of reasoning in morality comes from the social domain – some moral principles are products of our needs and interests as social beings. Practical decisions, on this view, are connected, again non-syllogistically, to accounts of one's role within given social communities. The moral decisions we make will be continually revised in our conversations with our colleagues, friends and others. I have emphasised, in the previous chapter, the importance of what I called 'emancipatory values' and their interlinking with the overcoming of subjugation. But working out what other values are important and worthy of being upheld will be a process of developing awareness of the economic, social and cultural conditions that influence our identities, our needs and desires.

On this outlook, a kind of practical reasoning is being used. On the Kohlbergian notion of reason, feeling is excised from moral decision making and immoral behaviour is described as that which allows for the domination of feelings over reason. A man who rapes, for example, is viewed as acting immorally because he is swayed by feeling instead of reason.

On the perspective of practical reason, by contrast, what is immoral about the man's behaviour is his choice of end; he acted as though he believed it is all right to rape. His behaviour, therefore, is immoral not because his reason failed to control his desires, but because he did not have the right kind of desire.

On this view of morality, whilst there may be some moral principles that derive from our sexed natures, it will not follow that there is a 'men's' and a 'women's' morality. It will not follow first because it will be important for both sexes to take heed of values that derive from the needs of the other sex: if there are, for example, legitimate moral principles that derive from the needs of women facing premenstrual tension, then both sexes must take them into account. But, second, I am suggesting that some principles will derive from the various 'communities' in which people are located; and many of these communities will be comprised of people of both sexes.

Practical Reason and Morality

Is it true, though, as many feminist critics have argued that it is, that what is wrong with the 'masculinist' Kohlbergian liberal morality is its attachment to a disembodied, disembedded subject? The answer to this question is: yes and no. The alienated notion of reason is linked with the disembodied subject in the following way: the subject that is 'pure mind' or 'pure reason', the classical Cartesian self, is by definition a disembodied and disembedded one. However, when it comes to applying the two notions in the moral domain, it is, I believe, the model of reason, and not the attenuated self, which is more appropriately the main target of criticism. For when we come to look at actual examples, such as Jake's, of liberal masculinist moral thinking, we find that the individuals concerned are not really 'abstracting' the self that is the object of the moral judgement from its context and its body. On the contrary, only if the person concerned has some particular distinguishing characteristics can moral principles be applied to particular instances. This is just one example, but, after all, the essence of the moral procedure in question is that of applying principles in particular cases, so it is just a caricature of liberal theory to suggest that it abstracts wholly from particular circumstances. And the feminist claim, correlatively, that there is a contradiction at the heart of liberal theory is derived, to a certain extent, from a caricature of that theory. To that extent, then, the answer to the question: is it true that liberal theorists, in their moral thinking, deploy the abstract, disembedded and disembodied self? is 'no'.

Yet, as Jean Grimshaw has argued, it is nonetheless true that the kind of reasoning process illustrated by the case of Jake, does present a too attenuated, an insufficiently rich picture of the real moral issue. The girl in the Gilligan experiment, when presented with the same example, appeared just to ramble, to present a mass of arguments that did not seem to cohere well together. Yet her position could, in fact, be characterised, in Grimshaw's way, as one which brings a wider range of principles to bear on the matter, some arguments in favour of each principle, and some means of attaining each. Her position, in other words, could be argued to be deploying a richer, more appropriate concept of reason.

Rather than adopting a postmodern response to Kohlberg, therefore, I would advocate developing a richer notion of reason and of emotion. This notion of reason can be associated, contrary to Gilligan, both with women and with men. I'd like to go on to argue, now, that an important moral principle is the notion of autonomy. I would like to argue that autonomy does not have to be associated with the 'narrow' conception of reason.

Autonomy

Postmodern feminists have subjected the concept of autonomy to critical scrutiny. In his famous 1984 essay, Fredric Jameson argued that the concept of autonomy is bound up with the bourgeois individual subject which is, according to him, not only a thing of the past, but also a myth.[10] Autonomy, he suggests, is an impossible notion, connected with the Cartesian attempt to conceptualise the self. The self, he argues, as you will, no doubt, have come to expect by now, is decentred and fragmented.

Another writer, Patricia Waugh, extends this critique of the concept of autonomy, suggesting that the autonomous subject of Enlightenment thought has excluded women.[11] (Some women have argued further that it excludes the interdependence that is important in the extended family.) But unlike Jameson, Waugh is sceptical both about the fragmented self of postmodernism and about the Enlightenment autonomous self. She suggests, indeed, in line with my earlier argument, that both, in their separating out of reason and feeling, are products of the same cultural tradition. The Enlightenment self is a transcendent rationality which splits from the emotional; the postmodern schizophrenic self is the *fin-de-siècle* parody, or caricature, of that dualism. Waugh is drawing, here, on a conception of the postmodern self which is partly inspired by the Freudian notion of the desire to destroy that which we cannot possess, itself producing a fragmented self.

Before moving to outline a conception of autonomy which, I hope, escapes these criticisms, I would like to make a couple of preliminary points. First of all, the Kantian self, which is the self to which one usually appeals for an account of Enlightenment autonomy, develops out of a critique of the Cartesian self. Kant argues that the Cartesian self cannot provide the conditions for self-knowledge that, he suggests, we do in fact have. Here again, we have evidence of a postmodernist associating the liberal humanist subject with only one manifestation of it – the Cartesian one. Secondly, it sometimes appears as though some postmodernist sympathisers believe that if there are problems with the Cartesian self, it follows that the self is fragmented and non-unitary. The latter claim may be true, but it doesn't follow from the fact that there are problems with Cartesianism. There is no obvious reason, as we have seen in Chapter 4, why we cannot both accept the fragmentary self and maintain some form of humanism.

I would now like to offer a brief account of autonomy which, I hope, circumvents some of the above objections. The account does not claim to be original, but it does, I hope, show that autonomy need not be viewed as Waugh, for example, does.

One sense of autonomy, in Kant's moral theory, is associated with the 'narrow' conception of reason: autonomy is pure, narrowly conceived rationality. To be autonomous, in this sense, a person has to be a purely rational self, unmoved by inclination. However, there is another strand to Kant's theory which can, I believe, more easily be defended. (As Jessica Benjamin has put it: 'our politics must find a form of transcendence which does not repudiate immanence, the ties that give and maintain life.'[12])

In this other strand of his theory, Kant instructed us to 'treat humanity, whether in your own person, or that of any other, never simply as a means, but always at the same time as an end'.[13]

People deliberate all the time about their wants and beliefs: some wants, for example the wish not to get lung cancer, may override others, for example the desire to smoke a cigarette. People are not subject to the necessity of nature. Men and women are not simply subject to their (unconsidered) desires; they can rationally reflect on those desires. One important part of the notion of autonomy, therefore, is impartially reflecting on one's wants and desires, and reviewing those desires in the light of moral principles and values. One is treating oneself as an end in the Kantian sense and not as a means if one 'makes one's will as one wants it to be'.[14] This is analogous to the Aristotelian process of becoming a virtuous person: the person whose desires have resulted from virtue.

Treating a person as an end, further, involves acting out of a disposition to seek out the best way of behaving, and this involves discussion and interaction with others. If I can ascertain whether or not I am behaving in a racist way in my treatment of a particular person, discussion with other people – particularly with other black people – will help me formulate appropriate principles and appropriate desires. Discussion with others may not remove all potential constraints on my acting autonomously: some constraints are economic, or grounded in physiology. For instance, a Nottinghamshire coal miner in the early 1980s may not have wanted to continue to work in the mines, yet he may have preferred that to the option on offer, of redundancy. But getting together with others, discussing the constraints on his situation, and then formulating principles on which to act, are stages in the process of changing the situation. Even where the constraints on autonomy appear to be outside the individual's control, there are steps that can be taken to alleviate the situation, if not for him personally, then potentially for others in that situation.

There are two aspects of autonomy, then, which I would argue are very important in any morality. First of all, there is the notion of autonomy as careful reflection, in the light of relevant information, on one's wants and desires; and secondly, and relatedly, there is autonomy as impartiality in the review of one's moral principles and values. Impartiality does not mean 'absolute' impartiality, in Kant's sense of treating everyone as attenuated rational agents, but it means attempting to take the needs of as many 'others' as possible into account, in determining appropriate moral principles. The ultimate decision as to what to believe, however, should be one's own. A further aspect of autonomy, I would argue, involves the right to make decisions about matters that are of deep moral concern to oneself, without being bribed, or being given deliberately distorted information. And this point applies to oneself as well: a person's responses to problems should be guided by rational decisions, and not by ill informed prejudices or by irrational impulses which they are unable to justify.

This conception of autonomy, rather than viewing the individual as an isolated 'rational' being, recognises the network of relationships and dependencies in which individuals are bound up. Like Foucault's description of the Enlightenment, I would emphasise the 'moment when humanity is going to put its own reason to use, without subjecting itself to any authority'.[15] Every individual is both critically independent, and caught up in a network of socio-cultural norms and ideals. A commitment to autonomy does not negate this undoubted truth about human interaction. Furthermore, it recognises that certain kinds of interaction are valuable in the pursuit of non-oppressive goals, whilst other types are repressive in this context. Autonomy involves both critical reflection on the desires and moral principles of others, and reflection on one's own motivations and behaviours.

McNay on Foucault on Autonomy

In an interesting reading of Foucault, Lois McNay has argued recently that Foucault, despite often being labelled an anti-Enlightenment thinker, in his later works on sexuality, offers a 'modern ethics' of the self, which provides for a rethinking of the notion of autonomy for feminists. She argues that Foucault sees in ancient Greek ethics a 'potential model for an ethics of existence for the modern individual'.[16] Foucault, she argues, believes that contemporary society has reached such a degree of scepticism about large-scale systems of belief that it must seek a more individualised basis for modern morality. Foucault draws both on Kant, the Kant of *What is Enlightenment?* and on Baudelaire, who makes of 'his body, his behaviour, his feelings and his passions, his very existence, a work of art'.[17] McNay argues, quoting John Rajchman, that Foucault rejects one aspect of Enlightenment thought: 'the linking of moral codes to a global perspective which is generally a notion of universal reason'.[18] However, instead of opting for a richer notion of rationality, along the lines I have suggested above, Foucault argues that there are multiple, historically specific types of rationality: 'I do not believe in a kind of founding act whereby reason, in its essence, was discovered or established. . . . I think in fact that reason is self created.'[19] McNay argues that Foucault's ethics furthers the modern ethical tradition, initiated by Sartre: 'Its principle is freedom, but a freedom which does not follow from any postulation of our nature or essence.'[20]

I am very sympathetic to some parts of this re-reading of the notion of autonomy, but I am sceptical about other aspects of it. A morality which is not underpinned by any attachment to particular ends or virtues runs the risk of not being a morality at all. A self that continually re-creates itself (as I have argued earlier) may not be in a position to establish any commonalities at all with other people, and may not, therefore, be in a position to describe common sources of, and ways of overcoming, oppression. I go along partly, although not wholly, as we have seen, with Foucault and McNay's desire to separate the attachment to particular ends from views of human nature – whether it be human nature or women's nature – but an alternative, I have been arguing, is to regard people as coming together – in 'communities' – because of their commitment to particular ends or 'virtues'.

Another feminist writer, Jessica Benjamin, has offered a view of autonomy which bears some resemblance to the above, in that she advocates a rethinking of the relation between autonomy and the network of relationships in which an individual is embedded. However, following Horkheimer, she argues that the intimate relations between mother and child, in the early bourgeois family, provide a model for a necessary component of autonomy: a commitment to the freedom and growth of the 'other'. 'What is nurturance if not the pleasure in the other's growth?'[21] The love of the mother-bond allows one to be 'known and respected for who you are, as well as who you can become'.[22] Whilst I concur with Benjamin's insistence on respecting people 'for who they are', I would not accept her appeal to the nurturant mother-love as the means for achieving this end. Mothering can be oppressive as well as caring and nurturant. A better role model for learning 'who the other really is' is a community of adults committed to the principles of autonomy articulated above. Moreover, it is not so much finding out 'who the other is' that is important, discovering their identity, as learning what key principles and desires inform their lives. This process may be an incredibly difficult one, yet it is the commitment to the principle that one ought to attempt to do it, that is important.

I would like to stress, once more, the commitment to attempting to uncover, in the ways articulated above, shared values and implementing them, rather than the Foucauldian commitment to a continual re-creation of identity. It may not be possible to speak of any clear-cut identity, because identities may be imposed or culturally inscribed. Identity based on norms of heterosexuality, where the assumption is made that everyone is either masculine or feminine, is a case described by recent feminists, as we have seen in the work of Judith Butler. Rather than emphasising autonomy as continual self-creation and re-creation, I would emphasise autonomy as continual commitment to re-evaluating one's desires and values, in the light of critical interaction with others. Political action is based not on shared identity, but on a critical adherence to shared values and beliefs: on the notion of a community of individuals sharing ends in common.

This notion of autonomy connects with attempts within modern critical theory to redeem the humanistic spirit of the Enlightenment project. Pauline Johnson points out that the masculinist instrumental notion of reason identified earlier with Kohlberg is, in fact, a deformation of the emancipatory, humanistic Enlightenment project.[23] She argues that Cassirer points out in his classic *The Philosophy of the Enlightenment* that eighteenth century thought was in part known for its commitment to the practical import of human reason. The instrumental view of reason, identified earlier in Kohlberg and Kant, was actually a deformation of that. The conception of autonomy I have outlined can contribute, I hope, to the project of reviving the humanistic spirit of the Enlightenment, and it is not associated with the negative view of the self – as pure transcendental reason – that Waugh, for example, connected it with.

Furthermore, it need not follow that an autonomous self must be a whole, unified non-fragmented self. The autonomous self, in the sense articulated, can have unconscious desires and wishes; it can have desires whose form and whose objects may be transformed.

7
Essentialism and Universalism Revisited

In Chapters 5 and 6, I have argued against the wholesale use of the notion of a female identity or a female nature to ground an epistemology or a morality. I have expressed scepticism about the notion of a 'women's epistemological standpoint' or a women's morality. However, there are two other areas where I would urge that the notion of nature be revived: one is in the analysis of the concept of woman (which has itself come in, as we have seen, for critical scrutiny from postmodernists and others), and the other is the understanding of 'patriarchy' or women's oppression.

We saw, in Chapter 1, that many contemporary, postmodernist influenced feminists are critical of universalising 'essentialist' feminisms. There are said to have been many types of such theory (although as we now know, some of these claims must be treated with a certain amount of scepticism). There are the biological accounts, such as that of Shulamith Firestone or some ecofeminists, which take women's oppression to arise out of some biological feature; there are the socialist-feminist perspectives, from Engels through to Delphy or Fergusson, according to which certain types of social system necessarily give rise to exploitation; there are the liberal theories, from Wollstonecraft through to de Beauvoir, which take oppression to be caused by the association of 'woman' with nature, the body and the emotions, whilst 'man' is rational, autonomous and human. There are also those theories, for example that of Nancy Chodorow, which see the cause of women's oppression to lie in some feature of women's experience – for example women's mothering. And there is, as we have seen, that type of feminism which sees oppression as arising from the 'phallocentric' character of the symbolic. In each case, the solution to the problem is either to advocate the valorisation of the quality or qualities which cause exploitation, as, for example, does Mary Daly, or some other ecofeminists, or to alter the feature in women or in society that gives rise to oppression. Thus, liberal feminists suggest that women take on the characteristics traditionally associated with masculinity; Irigaray and others advocate the creation of a new symbolic system; socialist feminists argue for the removal of social conditions which give rise to oppression; and some of the biologically inclined feminists suggest that we change our biology!

As we have seen in earlier chapters, universalising feminisms, particularly the biological, the liberal and those which see the key feature to be some aspect of women's *experience*, have been extensively criticised. Objections to them, as we have seen, encompass the following:

1. There are no universal features or experiences that all women share. The supposition that there are is ideological, in that it involves the protagonist in generalising features of her own era, culture, experience, to all women. Some even go so far, as we have seen in the case of Butler, as to deny that there is such a concept as 'woman'.
2. Universalising feminisms lead to a misguided essentialism.
3. Universalising feminisms mistakenly hypostatise some actual or potential state where exploitation and oppression will have disappeared. But this outlook is heavily Utopian; it assumes that there is progress in history, when this assumption has been shown, by events like the holocaust (Lyotard) and by recent readings of past events/discourses (Foucault) to be outmoded.

I shall attempt to respond to some of these critical points in this chapter.

I hope it will not seem pedantic to rehearse again the main reasons why feminists proposed universalising theories. The first point to make is that feminism itself came about because of such theories. The label 'feminist' was deployed, in the second wave of feminism, to describe women who came together because of a belief in shared oppression. Women came together as women, not as black women or women with disabilities, because of a belief that men were, in Delphy's words, the 'main enemy'.[1] These women disagreed as to why men took on this role: some believing that they did so by nature, others because of unconscious drives/desires, yet others because of social conditions. But all agreed on one thing, that women were oppressed as women. They shared this view with earlier feminists like Simone de Beauvoir or, much earlier still, Mary Wollstonecraft. Contemporary critics of universalising feminisms may be using the word 'feminist' illegitimately if there is no shared oppression. Many postmodernist influenced women would indeed forgo the use of this label. Others, however, deploy the category while overtly rejecting it: those who argue that the most one can do is account for local forms of sexism such as providing an explanation of some racist and sexist characteristics in the Hispanic community of Harlem in the 1960s, for example, must deploy the general concept. Those who do forgo the use of the label, indeed, may be on the slippery slope to abandoning the use of all terms indicating common sources of and forms of oppression. The strategy, then, may be conservative and individualist in effect.

In this chapter, I would like to offer a defence of two unfashionable claims: a kind of essentialism, and a form of universalism. I will suggest, though, that the question of whether or not it is possible to define 'woman', whether there are qualities that all women share, can and should be separated from the question of whether women are oppressed as women.

The Sex–Gender Distinction

My argument rests on a defence of the sex/gender system, a distinction that has itself come in for extensive criticism recently. In the 1970s, it was criticised by anti-feminist, biological arguments, and in the 1980s by feminists. I would like to look, first, at some of the former arguments.

Some Biological Arguments

There have been several attempts in the past to reduce 'gender' to biological sex. In the late nineteenth century, in Britain and elsewhere, theories about natural sex differences were used to justify differential treatment of the sexes. For instance, the supposed science of 'craniology' (the study of the brain size) correlated women's supposedly less highly developed frontal lobes (said to be the site of intellectual ability) with 'natural' nurturing qualities, domesticity, passivity and affection.[2]

In the same period, another argument from the premise that the sexes are naturally different was used to refuse women access to higher education. As the evolutionary philosopher Herbert Spencer, writing in 1867, put it: 'the deficiency of reproductive power among upper class girls may reasonably be attributed to the overtaxing of their brains – an overtaxing which produces a serious reaction on the physique.'[3]

At the turn of the century, neuro-anatomists decided that it was the parietal lobes, and not the frontal ones, that were the site of the intellect. 'Natural "gender" differences' were soon accommodated to this shift in theory. Here is Ruth Bleier on the subject: 'It did not take long for the leading anatomists of the period to "discover" that women's parietal lobes were *not* really larger and their frontal lobes smaller than men's . . . but quite the reverse.'[4]

Biological determinists' accounts of gender go in and out of fashion; indeed it is possible that the waxing and waning of interest in them at particular points in time is related to fluctuations in the economy. It certainly appeared in the 1980s, in the US and increasingly in Britain, that the re-emergence of the belief that it is women's natural role to be a mother was connected with the increase in unemployment, and the need, on the part of governments, to mask the extent of that phenomenon. If the woman's role lies in the home, she does not appear to be out of work, and she therefore does not figure in unemployment statistics. Similarly, but for a different reason, immediately after the Second World War, the appearance of a spate of books on the naturalness of motherhood for women, corresponded with the return on the job market of the men who came back from war.

Today, biological arguments for the determination of gender identity are fashionable in far right political circles. For instance, the British National Front views attempts to alter the relation between the sexes as misguided because the biology that underpins gender inequalities cannot be changed. For example: 'One only has to observe the degree to which male dominance and female passivity in sexual courtship obtains in the animal world, likewise qualities of male aggression and female domesticity, to understand their fundamental biological basis.'[5]

Sociobiology

In 1975, one of the most prominent writers on sociobiology, E. O. Wilson, sought to establish it as 'the systematic study of the biological basis of all social behaviour'.[6] Wilson believes that all human behaviours are genetically evolved adaptations. Dawkins, author of the popular book on sociobiological theory, *The Selfish Gene*, puts the point more starkly. For him, human beings are robot vehicles blindly programmed to preserve the selfish molecules known as genes.[7]

Wilson argues that particular behaviours evolve through genetic adaptations, based on natural selection. 'Successful' or adaptive behaviours become, he believed, based on our genes; certain genetic combinations are selected because they produce those behaviours. The behaviours become human *nature*. And human nature, for men, is made up of the characteristics of *masculinity*. As Wilson puts it: 'Males are characteristically aggressive towards one another and most intensely during the breeding season. . . . Included in male "nature" is male dominance: universal male dominance is a fact of nature'.[8]

Women's nature is, by contrast and not unexpectedly, feminine: it is more profitable for females to be coy, to hold back until they can identify males with the best genes.[9] Van den Berghe and Barash, also sociobiologists, say this: 'Males and females are selected for differing patterns of parental care, and there is no reason to exempt homo sapiens from this generalisation.'[10]

Thus, different responsibilities for parental care on the part of the two sexes are part of human nature. Women and men are apparently *naturally* feminine and masculine, and this comes about because so being is the best way that each sex secures the reproduction of its genes. But, as Ruth Bleier and others have argued, there is a circularity in the reasoning of Wilson and Barash here. They have selected certain dispositions to act (for example the differing responsibilities of the two sexes for parenting) as pieces of behaviour that have been adapted to survive. They then construct a story to show how the behaviour contributes to the reproductive success of the individual; and, as Bleier puts it, 'this *conjecture* then becomes evidence for the *premise* that the behaviour was genetically determined.'[11] The implication of Bleier's point is that the behaviours are arbitrarily chosen – that any of a potentially very large list of types of behaviours *could* have been offered as the one to be genetically explained – and the justification for this arbitrary choice is, in fact, circular.

This is an important point, for sociobiologists pick out sexually differentiated 'traits' like coyness (in women), promiscuity (in men), or maternalism (in women) and describe these as human nature. But if there is no non-circular justification for selecting these qualities, then there is no ground for the sociobiologists' claim that these constitute human nature.

A central argument in some sociobiological theory, and this point appears in Dawkins and in Wilson, is that males and females have different strategies for going about the maximisation of their individual genes' ability to reproduce themselves. These different strategies constitute, for the sociobiologist, different natures in men and women. Since men can reproduce millions of sperm a day, a male can theoretically produce enough sperm to service a harem of females. Thus, they argue, men's method of securing the maximum reproduction of their genes will be to inseminate as many women as possible. Further, their relative investment in any one woman will be small. A woman, they say, on the other hand, will attach a lot more significance to each one of her children, because her eggs are much larger than sperm and therefore take longer to produce; she only produces one egg at a time and far fewer eggs than a man does sperm in a lifetime; she is capable of producing only one child a year. So, although the *genetic* contribution of each parent to the child is equivalent (twenty-three chromosomes each), the woman invests a lot more of her reproductive potential in each child. Therefore, different behaviours, amounting to different natures in women and men, are adapted to survive: males will be aggressive, fickle and undiscriminating; females coy and discerning.

Women, they argue, will go for long term relationships with one mate so as to ensure the best possible survival of their genes; men will go for having relationships with as many women as possible, in order to maximise the reproductive potential of their genes.

> Given the initial imbalance in investment, the male may maximise
> his chances of leaving surviving offspring by copulating with and
> abandoning many females. Whereas [in species that rear young]

it is [also] important for females to select more males who are
likely to stay with them after insemination.[12]

Earlier, following Bleier, I argued that the particular choice of behaviours
was *arbitrary*. Let us, therefore, see if we could not explain the need of
both females and males to maximise their respective reproductive potential by completely different behaviours. Indeed, let us hypothesise that the
behaviours of women and men are precisely the opposite of those assumed
to be characteristic by the sociobiologists. Let us suppose, that is, that
women are the ones who tend to maximise the number of partners they
have, whereas men tend to stay with one person. Could these behaviours
be justified sociobiologically? I suggest that they could. We could argue
that the woman chose to 'mate' with as many 'male' partners as possible
in order to maximise her chances of fertilising her precious egg. (Many
of her potential male 'partners', after all, may be infertile.) Indeed, after
she has succeeded in becoming pregnant, and given birth to her child, the
larger the number of partners, the better her chance of securing one who
is really good at helping care for the child.

I am pursuing this line of thought, not in order to justify these behaviours as part of our natures, but merely to point out that the sociobiologists have no good grounds for proclaiming the particular behaviours
they select to be part of female and male natures. On the contrary, such
behaviours are arbitrarily selected. Indeed, they are not just arbitrary; they
surely reflect, to quote Bleier again: 'naive ethnocentric, androcentric, and
anthropocentric fallacies'.[13] For instance, in order to justify their claims
for the universality of the properties they select as natural, they set out
to produce evidence of the existence of these qualities in the animal and
plant domain. Bleier argues, however, that the terms used are derived
from human behaviour to describe the behaviours outside this domain,
and that these are often inappropriate. An interesting example she quotes
is the description by Barash of the insertion of a pollen tube into a female
plant by the male flower as 'rape'. But, she says, it is implausible
that the female plant 'sees' the act as the result of violent, aggressive
behaviour on the part of the plant with the male flowers. In other words,
the description of the behaviour of the plant as 'rape' seems utterly inappropriate, and the sociobiologists' attempts to validate their claim that
such behaviour in human animals is part of their nature by producing
evidence from the plant domain are suspect.

A very different kind of perspective on sociobiological theory has been
articulated by Donna Haraway. She offers a fascinating postmodern
reading of sociobiological theory (or theories) as a 'narrative of biological meaning'.[14] She looks, amongst others, at the work of Hrdy, as a
sociobiologist and a feminist of a sort. Hrdy in *The Woman that Never
Evolved* argued that keeping males uncertain about paternity was an

advantage retained by females in an evolutionary strategy weighted towards the physical strength of men. Hrdy offers an evolutionary justification for the kind of female sexual promiscuity I suggested above could be justified on sociobiological premises. Female primates, according to her, 'influence males by consorting with them, thereby manipulating the information available to males about possible paternity' (Hrdy, in Haraway, p. 154). In her commentary on Hrdy, Haraway asks, provocatively: 'How did it come about that non-identity must mean competitive difference? And how did that original difference translate into cosmic limits on female power and agency?' (p. 155). 'Part of the answer, remote in time and non-negotiable – but not particularly satisfying – is *anisogamy*, from the Greek *aniso* (meaning unequal) plus *gametes* (eggs and sperm): gametes differing in size' (p. 155). Haraway playfully satirises: 'Whatever the merits of the tale, whose doubtfulness Hrdy signals even while invoking it in order to get her own narrative going, it is always satisfying to start an important origin story with a Greek etymology' (p. 156). Haraway's view, then, is that 'like it or not' sociobiologists 'write intertextually within the whole historically dynamic fabric of western accounts of development, change, individualism, mind, body, liberalism, difference, race, nature and sex' (p. 158).

Although I have been critical of some readings of sociobiological theory, I do not want to go so far as Haraway, for she is effectively denying the possibility of developing an objective human sociobiology. As MacIntyre, for instance, has argued, the claim that there is no evolved human nature has to be shown not to be itself a product of ideological prejudice.[15] I will argue, later in this chapter, in favour of retaining some notion of human nature. My critical discussion here, has been directed not against the notion of a women's nature, but against what I am suggesting maybe an inappropriate rendition of this nature.

The Feminist Critique of the Sex/Gender Distinction

I shall now present some of the *feminist* arguments against the sex/gender distinction. In the seventies, it became commonplace in feminist circles to argue that there is a distinction between one's 'sex' on the one hand and one's 'gender' on the other. Anne Oakley, in her famous book on the subject, put it thus: '"Sex" is a biological term; "gender" a psychological and cultural one'.[16] Michelle Barrett, in her book, *Women's Oppression Today*, saw 'sex as a biological category and gender as a social one'.[17] It became commonplace that 'sex' related to the biological characteristics of maleness or femaleness. One's sex could be identified at birth; it was a clear-cut matter, and could only be changed with difficulty. One's sex is a 'natural' phenomenon. Gender, on the other hand, is a psychological or cultural characteristic; it is not natural but acquired. Feminists, assuming that the equating of oppression with unchanging biological characteristics is misguided, then spent years working on different types of theory of the origins of gender identity: cognitive psychological, psychoanalytic, sociological, economic or some combination of these.

More recently, feminists have decried the dualism of such theories. They have objected to the metaphysical, Cartesian dualism implied by them, where mental, psychological characteristics are effectively privileged over bodily qualities, and where an interaction with 'others' takes place on a 'mental psychological plain'. They object, first of all, that such a picture just does not ring true – as Hegel pointed out, in *The Phenomenology of Spirit*, no characteristic is 'purely' mental; all of them have a bodily side to them. One cannot isolate thought and give it expression independently of its embodiment in a living subject.

Correlatively, it is not obvious that one can isolate the biological from the social or mental domain. First, it is not the case that the set of 'biological' criteria going to make up one's sex – chromosomes, genitalia, hormones and secondary sex characteristics – is present in the same way in every person. Some people are biologically 'neuter'. And apart from such cases, there is, in most people, variation in the characteristics. Women have varying amounts of oestrogen and testosterone. It is, moreover, logically possible for bodies to be categorised differently: some culture might identify more than two sexes as the norm, or differentiate bodies in other ways than by sex. No doubt, the cultural presumption that there are two genders influences one's perception of the biological criteria determining which sex a person is. As Alison Jaggar has pointed out, cultural criteria can influence the biological characteristics themselves. This phenomenon is evident in the case of contemporary female Olympic athletes, some of whom have attenuated female secondary sex characteristics.

But additionally, even supposing that one could isolate the mental from the bodily characteristics, it is argued that any privileging of the 'mental' 'psychological' aspect of a person, reinforces sexism by emphasising characteristics traditionally associated with masculinity – reason, thought, mental characteristics as opposed to those connected with femininity: bodily attributes.

Even if sex/gender theorists were not explicitly committed to metaphysical dualism, it is said that there is a kind of dualism that Alison Jaggar has labelled 'normative dualism' implied in their writings.[18] Sex/gender theorists, the critics say, are like contemporary liberal political theorists, who ascribe political rights on the basis of what they take to be the specifically human capacity for rationality, in their relative disregard for merely physical capacities and incapacities. Early liberal feminists, like Mary Wollstonecraft, advocated women being allowed to develop their 'rational' faculties, which, she thought, had been denied expression both by the social, educational and economic circumstances in which women found themselves, and by male political theorists writing about women's faculties. Sex/gender feminists, it is argued, whilst they are critical of liberal feminists for failing to recognise the deep-seated character of sexism, and for advocating change merely on an individual level, effectively embraced the same presuppositions, by denigrating the bodily domain.

The critics say, further, that feminists who advocate the sex/gender distinction presuppose, in Moira Gatens' words, an 'arbitrary' connection between femininity and the female body.[19] In contrast, Gatens argues that the subject is always a sexed subject. Patriarchy is, in her view, not a 'system of social organisation that valorizes the masculine gender over the feminine gender. Gender is not the issue; sexual difference is' (p. 145). Gatens describes herself as a 'difference' feminist; she is critical of those feminists who hypostatise the social or psychological manifestation of gender, and the effective elimination of masculinity and femininity as the 'solution' to patriarchy. Instead, she emphasises that any 'femininity' lived by a man, by someone with a male body, must be qualitatively different from femininity experienced by a person with a female body. Bodies are not – as she argues the sex/gender distinction assumes – neutral and passive; rather they are lived and located. Bodies also figure, she points out, as 'imaginary' bodies – bodies as lived by their inhabitants.

Gatens argues that the subjectivity of a male transsexual is qualitatively different from that of a female. The former's relation to his body is quite different. She argues that the male transsexual's primitive ego conflicts with his imaginary and biological body, leading to him seeing himself as female-in-a-male-body. She claims that this implies the non-resolution of his (mis)recognition of his mother's body for his own. *He* has never adequately separated from his mother.

Other feminists, recently, following Foucault (but in a critically sympathetic fashion), have set out to develop a theory of the gendered body and its emotions and needs that maintains its *materiality*, but that is not essentialist. Many feminists (see Butler, Plaza, Lois McNay) have pointed to the way in which the distinction between *genders* produces a sexed nature. Rather than sex being the primary edifice on which gender is constructed, gender informs and influences the categorisation of people as sexed. One example of this can be found in Simone de Beauvoir's work. She uses derogatory language to describe female sexual parts and sexual functions. For de Beauvoir, a woman's body is passive, not actively desiring, but passively evoking desire:

> [it] is not perceived as the radiation of a subjective personality, but as a thing sunk deeply in its own immanence; it is not for such a body to have reference to the rest of the world, it must be the promise of things other than itself; it must end the desire it arouses.[20]

When de Beauvoir describes the male sex organ, she uses adjectives that afford it positive value – 'the sex organ of a man is simple and neat as a finger'[21] – whilst the adjectives used to describe the female sex organ are negative:

> the feminine sex organ is mysterious even to the woman herself, concealed, mucous and humid, as it is; it bleeds each month, it is often sullied with body fluids, it has a secret and perilous life of its own ... feminine sex desire is the soft throbbing of a mollusc ... man dives upon his prey like the eagle and the hawk; woman lies in wait like the carnivorous plant, the bog, in which insects and children are swallowed. She is absorption, suction, humus, pitch and glue, a passive influx, insinuating and viscous.[22]

De Beauvoir is critical of the exclusion of the feminine from subjectivity, from the transcendence of the body. Yet the language she uses to describe the female body is infused with self-denigratory, 'phallocentric' metaphors. The penis is animated, a 'tool'; the vagina an 'inert receptacle.'[23] For the man, sexual intercourse is an 'outward relation to the world and others'; for the woman, intercourse can only be 'an interior event', 'a renunciation of her individuality for the benefit of the species'.[24] For de Beauvoir, 'woman, like man, is her body; but her body is something other than herself'.[25]

Recent feminists make explicit what is implicit in de Beauvoir. For Butler, for instance, drives are never pre-social: they are always produced within the social domain of gender. Developing themes in Foucault, other feminists have pointed to the various ways in which different discourses of power – for example, the discourses of the medical, psychiatric and educational institutions of the nineteenth century – have contributed to the hysterisation of the female body.

In this picture, oppression is based on the appropriation of women's bodies by patriarchy, but it does not derive from the body or sex. The female body and the feminine gender are therefore said to be 'not radically discontinuous'.[26] 'Gender is neither the causal result of sex nor seemingly fixed as sex.'[27] In other words, these feminists argue that one cannot distinguish 'sex' from 'gender' on the ground that sex is always gendered.

The objections to the sex/gender distinction from feminists then can be summarised as follows:

1. The body is not passive and neutral.
2. Gender cannot be manipulated at will, and it is not independent of the body – gender is not the causal effect of sex.

3. The body/mind dualism that underpins the distinction is misguided.
4. The distinction assumes a binary opposition between the sexes that may be heterosexist.
5. All biological characteristics are partly social and mental and social qualities partly bodily and biological.

I believe, however, that one does not need to uphold these claims in order to believe in the distinction. Indeed, it seems to me that protagonists of the distinction do not uphold them. I shall look at some of the case studies of one of the major advocates of the distinction, Robert Stoller, in order to illustrate this point.

Robert Stoller: A Re-Reading of the Sex/Gender Distinction

Stoller's major work *Sex and Gender* is a study of the multifarious influences upon a person's sexuality.[28] A substantial proportion of the book is devoted to the examination of the gender identity of individuals whose biological sex is indeterminate. This identity (starts with) 'the knowledge and awareness, whether conscious or unconscious, that one belongs to one sex and not the other' (p. 10). Stoller examines such people in order to shed light on the question: Is one's sense of oneself as belonging to a particular gender primarily biologically or psychologically and culturally caused? Stoller draws the distinction between 'sex' and 'gender' in the following way: 'To determine sex, one must assay the following physical conditions: chromosomes, external genitalia, internal genitalia (e.g. uterus, prostate), gonads, hormonal states and secondary sex characteristics' (p. 9). He adds the following bracketed addendum: '(It seems very likely that in the future another criterion will be added: brain systems.)'

The sexes are defined by 'the algebraic sum' of all qualities, and most people fall under one or the other head. There are also, however, 'certain amounts of overlapping in all humans' and, genetically speaking, there are other sexes: in addition to the XX female and the XY male, there are individuals with other chromosomal combinations – XO, XXY, XXXX, etc.

Gender, on the other hand, 'has psychological or cultural' rather than biological connotations.

I would like to look at some of Stoller's work, with a view to examining whether the above objections to the sex–gender distinction apply to it. I will begin with the first criticism: that the body is assumed, by advocates of the sex/gender distinction, to be passive and neutral.

One of Stoller's case studies runs as follows: a child who was thought at birth to be a normal female and was therefore brought up as a girl began behaving in 'masculine' ways. As a baby she was 'active and forceful'; as a child, when she played games she took male roles.

She could scarcely be forced into girls' clothes. . . . Her companions were boys, with whom she played boys' games . . . jumping, exploring, football. . . . When adolescence approached, she developed a cold with a hoarseness that persisted. Because of this change in voice she withdrew in great embarrassment from all social contacts and wanted to drop out of school.

She had a physical examination, and she was found to be:

a chromosomally normal male with a fully erectile tiny penis of clitoral size, hypospadias (a fissure in the lower wall of the male urethra – the result of a congenital malformation) bilateral cryptordism, bifid scrotum, and normal prostate. When finally told that [she] was, after all, a boy, she exhibited no surprise.

This case offers some evidence for a biological influence in gender formation, even though the case is not clear-cut for, as Stoller says: 'significantly, [he] has passed from being a mediocre to an excellent student. For example, he came to be among the first in his class in mathematics, a subject in which he had done very poorly when he thought he was a girl.'[29]

Although Stoller advocates social and psychological conditioning as significant determinants in gender identification, the 'body' is far from passive and neutral. Stoller argues that there is a 'biological force' contributing to a person's core gender identity, which may, in rare cases, be strong enough to contradict both anatomy and social conditioning. The biological force, Stoller suggests, acts, in rare cases, to influence one's unconscious identification as masculine or feminine. This force is not equivalent in everyone: it may have a greater effect, he argues, in some people than in others.

Rather than being 'passive and neutral' the body plays a major and active role in Stoller's work both in an individual's self-perception as belonging to a particular gender, and in the ascription by others to a person of a particular gender identity. In certain cases, there appears to be a very strong biological pull in a particular direction which seems to run counter to any other qualities that go to make up a particular gender. For instance, the discussion of a mother's worries about her daughter's masculinism runs:

The child ate so fast. It wasn't like a little girl. . . . As a tiny baby she moved too fast. She did everything crash! Bang! Nothing gentle. . . . I don't recall her ever sitting down with a book, except taking a magazine and fling it over the floor and look in the pages and page through it and tear it – *violently*. (Stoller, p. 68)

(It turns out that the 'girl' was biologically male.) Many of us today would, no doubt, question the mother's supposition that these are *masculine* qualities (and the assumption that little girls, and not little boys, sit down quietly and read books). However, they illustrate the very strong role played by the biological body in Stoller's writings.

On the second of the criticisms: that sex–gender theorists assume that gender is the causal effect of sex, again some of Stoller's case studies illustrate that he does not take this view. One of Stoller's case studies is someone who was chromosomally XO (instead of XX – female – or XY – male); at 18 'she' had no breasts and she never menstruated. Yet, Stoller claims that 'she' was 'quite unremarkably feminine in her behaviour, dress, social and sexual desires, fantasies.'[30]. In this case, the person identified as a woman, yet her biological make-up was chromosomally unlike most women.

Another patient of Stoller's was clearly female and feminine, despite the fact that she (also) was biologically neuter. Then in her teens, this person was told that her sex (as female) was genetically and anatomically incorrect, and she had, when Stoller saw her, 'gradually become psychotic'.[31]

Clearly, these cases illustrate that gender is not simply the causal effect of sex. As Stoller himself puts it: 'The cases discussed so far confirm that gender identity is created (*partly*) post-natally as a result of psychological influences' (my italics).[32]

On the third of the criticisms levelled against the sex/gender distinction – that gender cannot, as the advocates of the distinction assume, be manipulated at will – Stoller again does not appear to fall foul of the objection. On the contrary, the overriding impression one receives from his work is that one's gender identity is far too deeply entrenched for that. The consequence of any attempt at perceived manipulation, indeed, would be likely to be psychosis for the individual concerned.

The fourth criticism – that the distinction assumes a binary opposition between the sexes that may be heterosexist – also, in my view, does not obviously apply to Stoller's work, although he might be criticised for adopting a 'patrocentric' conception of social and psychological conditioning. One point that should be made is that, in his discussion of transsexuals, Stoller appears to attach an inordinate weight to the ways these individuals were treated, particularly by their mothers, in childhood. In these cases, he does not appear to pay the same attention as in other cases, to the range of possible influences on a person's sexuality and gender identification.

In many other cases, however, he is quite clear that there is the sort of influence advocated by some recent feminists. He says:

> core gender identity is produced, starting at birth, by three
> components. The first of these is the contribution made by the

anatomy of the external genitalia. By their natural appearance, the external genitalia serve as a *sign* to parents that the ascription of one sex rather than the other was correct. Then, too, by the production of sensation, the genitalia, primarily from external structures but in females additionally and duly from the vagina, contribute to a part of the primitive body ego, the sense of self, and the awareness of gender. The second component . . . is made up of the parents' expectations of the child's gender identity. . . . The third component is the postulated *biological force*. (pp. 72–73)

Stoller spends some considerable time questioning what he, and others, saw as the 'androcentric bias' in Freud's theory of the acquisition of gender identity. He argues, *contra* Freud, that core gender identity is present from earliest life and that the penis is not essential for the male's sense of masculinity. He argues a parallel case for the girl – that her sense of gender identity derives, in a precisely parallel way to that of the boy, from the three features mentioned above: anatomical features, the way she is treated by her parents, and biological sources. A girl's sense of herself as gendered, he suggests, is generally a non-traumatic learning experience (as taken for granted by the infant as her learning that she has only one head, two eyes, a mouth and so on) (p. 50). Stoller spends some time quoting extensively from the work of Karen Horney and Ernest Jones, who are critical of what they perceive to be the masculine bias of Freud's writing. He also mentions favourably, in a footnote 'the impressive work by Bettelheim, *Symbolic Wounds*, which reviews anthropological data demonstrating men's envy and fear of women's tenderness' (p. 52). As with the penis for the boy, Stoller claims that the vagina is not the essential source of femininity for the girl.

Stoller quotes Freud's famous view to the effect that a woman's sense of what is ethically normal is different from that of a man; that the superego is never so inexorable, so independent of its emotional stigma in a girl as in a boy and that women show less of a sense of justice than men. He says, of Freud's claim, that such opinions must stand or fall on demonstrable evidence 'no longer buttressed by the theory that women are by nature inferior to men, their personalities simply variants on the theme of their being castrated males' (p. 60).

Stoller emphasises that one of his central disagreements with Freud is that he, Freud, misses out on an early stage of gender acquisition; he suggests that Freud's emphasis on the 'phallic stage' in sexuality as the primary stage in the acquisition of gender identity is misguided. Stoller refers to a phase in the girl's life, prior to the Freudian Oedipal phase, a phase 'before tenderness has been depreciated' (p. 63).

It might be argued, however, that Stoller's view that there is a primary gender imprinting process that occurs very early on in the child's life makes him, in fact, more prone to the accusation of a heterosexist binary division between the sexes. At least, one could argue, Freud saw the acquisition of gender identity to be a complex psychological process. Stoller, by contrast, sees 'core' gender identity, with its attendant patrocentric baggage, to be unproblematically acquired early on in life. However, a point that should be made on the other side is that Stoller places less emphasis than Freud on the role of sexual drives and instincts in the acquisition of gender identity. The charge of *hetero*sexism was made by Butler against Freud because of the character of the *sexual* drives he is supposed to have assumed (see Chapter 1).

In the final analysis, it is almost impossible to prove that a particular way of drawing the distinction between the sexes and/or the genders absolutely is or is not sexist or heterosexist. I have given some evidence that Stoller's is not. Those who remain unconvinced may be unconvinced that any ways of drawing the distinction, in 'symbolic systems' that are androcentric, are free of bias.

As for the fifth objection, again I think that Stoller would accept that biological qualities are partly social: indeed, most of the case studies he documents concern the effects of 'social' identification as male or female, on the basis of rudimentary biological evidence. Everyone whose case he considered was identified as belonging to a particular sex, at birth, on the basis of apparent external genitalia, even where these genitalia appeared to be unusual. The identification as 'male' and 'female', therefore, was based on minimal biological evidence, and on the social expectation that the external genitalia indicated membership of a certain sex.

Additionally, Stoller documents the effects of possible social interventions in biological phenomena, for example, castration, the administration of oestrogen to men and androgens to women.

Arguments in Favour of the Sex/Gender Distinction

There are at least four reasons, in my view, why the distinction between 'sex' and 'gender' serves a useful purpose. First, we can distinguish, to take one example, that of mothering, the person who gives birth to a child, the biological mother, from the one who nurtures it – the social or psychological mother. Indeed, recent debates over surrogacy have made this distinction all the more clear-cut. A parallel distinction can be drawn in the case of females, between qualities which identify them as biologically female, and those culturally varying characteristics which identify a person as feminine. Second, as Plumwood argues, the distinction between the class of females and the set of characteristics associated with them (one version of the distinction) is essential to explaining how it is that philosophy (and contemporary areas such as public life) has been androcentric.[33]

The distinction allows us to say, for example, that Plato allows females in the Guardian class, but devalues the feminine. Third, as we have seen in the discussion of sociobiology, the distinction has been a major weapon in the battle against biological reductionism. And, finally, the distinction has served an important political point. It has allowed one to express reservations about some of the trappings of masculinity without necessarily criticising biological males.

'Sex'

I would argue, then, that there is a distinction to be drawn between sex and gender. The 'sex' side is characterised by a minimal notion of the body; by the set of minimally necessary biological factors that enable us to identify a particular body as male or female. It is understood, as has already been argued, that these biological features need not be unchanging (they can be altered by either psychological or social 'manipulation') nor are they present in the same quantities in every male or in every female. There is, however, a minimally necessary set of bodily or biological features present in every female, features the presence of which enables us to identify the person as female. This set will consist in some combination of chromosomes, hormones, genitalia and secondary sex characteristics. This forms the 'real essence' or the nature of the kind 'female' in something closely akin to a Lockean sense. The real essence properties of a kind being essential does not imply that they are fixed by nature. A particular set of properties may be essential at one time but not at another. In this sense, then, I would argue in favour of 'essentialism' about women.

None of the above underplays the very important work that feminists have been carrying out on the body, following Foucault's repositioning of it in social and historical analysis. Many feminists' concepts of the body are both richer and more culturally varying than the notion I am describing here. Nevertheless, the significance of Stoller's work, I would argue, lies in the detailed attention he gives to this minimal notion of the body, and the social and psychological effects on a person who has a different 'minimal' body from most men and women. His work suggests, indeed, how significant this minimal body is in influencing social and psychological identity. The descriptions he gives of minimally sufficient biological conditions for the ascription of maleness and femaleness are culturally inscribed: in the significance attached by the doctor who identifies the person at birth as male or female; in the social significance of the occupancy of one or the other body. In this sense, gender can be said to be the apparatus of production whereby the sexes are established. And yet, in another sense, this is going too far. This claim is only true to the extent that any set of decisions about categorisations is socially and culturally inscribed. The decision to divide up one's room in one set of ways rather than another rests on a choice, that is influenced by layers of history and culture; yet it is also, I have argued in Chapter 3, based on what is really there in the room. Similarly, if we go too far down the Foucauldian road, in the instance under discussion, we risk eliminating a basis for categorising human beings that is sensible, and politically useful in many instances. In this sense, strategic essentialism and the view that 'we cannot afford not to be essentialist' if we are interested in sexual difference, is based on real differences between men and women.[34]

But further, there will be some normative consequences of the foregoing. In the previous chapter, I argued for an approach to morality that is partly humanist, in the sense that values emerge from human interests, desires and concerns. These values are arrived at, I suggested, by means of a process of critical reflection on one's desires, informed by recognition of the importance of the ends and desires of others.

However, additionally, as I also argued in the previous chapter, some values will be derived from a consideration of male and female natures: it will be imperative to defend both the conditions for the survival of these natures, and the conditions for their flourishing. Naturalistic feminism, in other words, will be a part of morality. I do not believe that any given set of 'natural needs' deriving from sexed natures can be clearly specified, nor that they will invariably play an overriding role in any moral decision making. But natural nature will play some role in determining appropriate ends.

Postmodern and Foucauldian influenced feminists properly stress the multi-faceted and layered nature of sexual difference. Many black women, for example, have different histories in relation to slavery and forced labour from many white women. Even the generalisation 'black women', as Spivak points out, glosses over substantial variations, for example, amongst different groups of 'Indian women'.[35] The concept of 'black woman' is itself, in part, a construction of the powerful white woman. And yet, just as the concept 'black woman' serves, for many black women, an important strategic and political function, so too, I have been arguing, does the concept 'woman'. And this strategic and political essentialism is partly grounded in a real bodily essentialism.

'Gender'

What, however, is meant by 'gender'? Gender, I would argue, is the social, psychological or cultural story of the body; it is the social or psychological view of sexual difference. It combines a set of culturally inscribed qualities – the set that culture identifies as characterising 'femininity' or 'masculinity' – and the individual's self-identification as belonging to a particular sex (whether or not that person is aware of the set of cultural characteristics).

De Beauvoir's notion that 'one is not born but *becomes* woman', can be read in two ways, then: individuals construct themselves as gendered, and society constructs them that way. Gender is not just stamped on bodies; rather individuals are, to an extent, free to construct themselves in particular ways.

Thus someone could identify as masculine in a culture influenced by the John Wayne image, without knowing about that image. So long as masculinity is not identified with any one set of characteristics, then it is compatible with the theory that it takes on different forms in varying cultural contexts.

In most known cultures, the particular social or psychological view of sex difference that has been adopted has embodied some 'sexist' characteristics (some characteristics that are oppressive to women): the examples of this are too numerous to describe and they have been extensively documented in the literature. The characteristics are, of course, culturally varying. Sexism, then, as well as women's biological nature, has been well nigh ubiquitous. However, it is possible to imagine non-sexist gender characteristics. These would be social or psychological qualities associated with a particular biological sex which just represented social or psychological differences without there being any implicit or explicit connotations of inequality.

Universalism

I would argue, then, in response to the critical points made at the outset of this chapter, that there are universal features which women share. It is also true that there has been a universal self-identification as masculine or feminine, on the basis of the possession of a particular type of sexed body. I have suggested, further, that some political or ethical consequences will flow from this universal identification as male or female. It will not follow, however, that one's identity as a woman will be a sufficient condition for all feminist projects and goals: only some political consequences will derive from one's nature as a woman.

A person's identity as a woman, therefore, does not conclusively determine her 'oppression', because, as well as being women, every woman is also something else: a lesbian philosophy lecturer, an African American lawyer or a white English cleaner. As well as these other aspects of one's identity, which will contribute to influencing the power relations into which we all fit, there are the various 'imagined' communities, outlined in Chapter 5, of which we are all members. Our membership of these communities will help determine our political and ethical priorities as much as our natures as men and women. My argument in this chapter, however, has invited a refocusing on nature and on the importance of the minimal biological body for providing a basis for a shared identity amongst women. The importance of this identity might, in certain circumstances, transcend the significance of other culturally inscribed or biologically based differences amongst women.

In certain circumstances, the characteristics I, as a white, middle class, heterosexual woman, share with my close Asian, Israeli and white English lesbian women friends, for example, transcend the differences between us. We support one another if one is suffering and we share laughs together. This sharing, of course, may have to do with something other than the fact that we are all women. Yet there are circumstances when that simple fact does seem to matter: once, when I was trekking in the Himalayas, I met a local Kashmiri woman. Seeing me dressed in my shorts and heavy walking boots she wanted to check, by touching my breasts, whether I was really a woman. Finding that confirmed, she and I appeared to reach some level of shared understanding.

The poststructuralists and postmodernists have taught us to be wary of false generalisation. The other side of the coin, however, is that in a world where difference sometimes leads to antagonism and antagonism to warfare, there are times when it is important to recognise our shared humanity and the shared concerns that may arise from that. There are other times, I am suggesting, when we may want to recognise, as women, the collective preoccupations that may arise from this fact about some of us.

8

A Critique of Constructivist Accounts of Sexuality

This chapter is concerned with a rather different subject: the theory of sexuality. Sexuality is not a topic that is usually taken to fall within the broad philosophical purview of earlier chapters of the book. Yet it is a subject that is central in psychoanalytic theory; it is one that has recurred on several occasions in the book, and it is also an issue that provides useful illustrative material of some of the debates covered elsewhere in the book. Moreover, it is a topic which, in much recent writing, has received a poststructuralist and a postmodernist reading. I would like, in this chapter, to offer a kind of 'essentialist' reading of the theory of sexuality.

Biological Determinisms

Much recent writing about sexuality could be said to be a kind of 'constructivism'. There is not, according to constructivists, speaking in a postmodern vein, 'a' sexuality, rather there are sexualities, constructed by a multiplicity of 'discursive practices'. Probably the best known 'constructivist' about sexuality is Foucault, but many writers, following Foucault, have expressed a similar point of view. I'd like to begin the chapter by explaining what it is that 'constructivists' about sexuality objected to.

In fact, constructivists about sexuality were motivated by several interlocking concerns. One fear was the spectre of biological determinism. This takes on varying forms depending on the vantage point from which the writer speaks. One of the earliest types of 'biological determinism' to which constructivists have objected sees sexuality as a 'drive-based sexologic'.[1] For Reich, sexuality is a universal biological drive, 'energy' that seeks satisfactory release.[2]

Freud, too, often assimilates sexual wishes or desires to biological drives that simply 'seek release'. He begins the *Three Essays on Sexuality*, for example, as follows: 'The fact of the existence of sexual needs in human beings and animals is expressed in biology by the assumption of a "sexual instinct", on the analogy of the instinct of nutrition.' In another passage, he says:

> Popular opinion has quite definite ideas about the nature and characteristics of the sexual instinct. It is generally understood to be absent in childhood, to set in at the time of puberty in connection with the process of coming to maturity and to be revealed in the manifestations of an irresistible attraction exercised by one sex upon the other; while its aim is presumed to be sexual union.[3]

The metaphor of the 'hydraulic model' is often used to describe Freud's view of sex drives. On this model, there is a constant supply of the 'sexual substance' which flows out through the mouth, the anus, the sex 'organs' and, on some readings of Freud, almost any other part of the body.

One aspect of the constructivists' critique of this view is that it gives an incorrect description of sexual desire. On the one hand, it is argued that it is not 'energy' or 'drives'; it is not 'released' through 'outlets'. But, on the other hand, constructivists have argued that the very language of 'energy' and 'drives' suggests its 'constructed' character. The language, it is perhaps interesting to note, contains a combination of metaphors from the science of hydraulics – sexuality is like water flowing through pipes – from the theory in physics of the constancy of the supply of energy, and from stimulus response theory in psychology/biology. No form of sexuality, in other words, is socially unconstructed or 'natural'. Rather, such theories often serve political and ideological functions. One biological theory that was commonplace in Victorian times was the view that human bodies in general contained a finite supply of energy. This theory was deployed to make the famous, highly political claim that women should not be educated, since energy used up in such a domain detracts from the 'proper' application of energy for women in childbearing and childrearing.[4]

More importantly than criticising the biological determinists' language as metaphor, however, constructivists have objected that the metaphors are thought to be taken too literally. The Victorian writers above believed in the literal truth of the claim that the human body is a kind of receptacle, containing a finite amount of energy, some of which is sexual. Constructivists have claimed that this picture of sexuality does not ring true. Sexual desires are not like drives or energy seeking release; rather they are only given meaning in social and cultural settings. There are two parts to this claim of the sexual constructivists: one is that any one sexual desire, expressed in a behavioural form, for example kissing, takes on a different meaning depending on whether you are Roman, Barbarian, ancient Greek or contemporary Asian.[5] The other is that theorists like Reich, Freud (sometimes) and Kinsey wrongly attempt to reduce *any* psychical, social, linguistic or cultural aspects of sexuality to a biological 'essence'. One part of the critique then is that any one behavioural manifestation of a sexual desire – for example, kissing – takes on a variety of forms and meanings; the other is that biological determinists set out (wrongly) to reduce the desire to some biological essence.

Another aspect of biological determinist theory to which some constructivists have objected is this: drive-based sexuality, even if it is not all there is assumed to be to sexuality, is somehow seen to be 'foundational' to any other form. Sexuality, on this version of the biological determinist viewpoint, may not be wholly to do with drives and 'outlets', but these drives are real, rather like Lockean real essences, whilst their counterparts – desires and wishes – are only the logical and causal effects of these 'outlets' and are somehow, therefore, less 'real'. Constructivists, by contrast, argue that sexual desires are not like this.

There is a further part to certain constructivists' rejection of 'biology'. This is a reaction against what they see as the over-reliance on the 'science' of biology in the study of matters sexual. A recent constructivist, Jeffrey Weeks, for example, traces the faith of many sexologists that, in the struggle between sexual ignorance and Enlightenment, biological and medical science would be the strongest weapon. He cites the case of Magnus Hirschfeld – a German sexologist – who saw his Berlin Institute seized and its papers burned by the Nazis, and yet who still proclaimed: 'I believe in science, and I am convinced that science, and above all the human sciences, must bring to mankind, not only truth, but with Truth, Justice, Liberty and Peace.'[6]

Sexual biology, so ran the belief – the study of instincts, brain centres, hormones, germ plasm, genes, and more recently vaginal blood flow and clitoral histochemistry – would provide nature's direction for human sexual conduct. Science would dictate the true nature of human sexuality.

Clearly, the Nazis thought differently about 'pure' objective science. Far from medical science being a strong weapon in favour of sexual liberation, its fruits were destroyed in one fell swoop. An over-reliance on science, in attempting to create an emancipatory discourse on sexuality then, may be inappropriate. But, additionally, Weeks argues that to focus on sexual desire and sexual pleasure as measurable states, is to paint both an inaccurate and a potentially mystificatory picture of the social and psychological aspects of sexuality. Again, here, it is the reductionist aspects of the physiological approach to sexuality which the constructivists describe as misleading.

There is a further aspect of the critique of biological determinism which emerges from recent feminist constructivist writing about sexuality. Several lesbian feminist writers have described the commitment, for example in psychoanalytic writing, to 'the institution of heterosexuality' (Sheila Jeffreys) as a form of biological determinism. For Monique Wittig, for example, psychoanalysis assumes heterosexuality to be a natural phenomenon. For her:

> there is no sex. There is but sex that is oppressed and sex that oppresses. It is oppression that creates sex and not the contrary. The contrary would be to say that sex creates oppression or to say that the cause (origin) of oppression is to be found in sex itself, in a natural division of the sexes pre-existing (or outside of) society.[7]

Any psychoanalytic theory, in other words, that purports to explain the production of self-identity and gendered difference is a type of biological determinist view, in so far as it presupposes a heterosexual mandate. Instead, Wittig advocates the abolition of the category of women and correspondingly new categories of person as materially oppressed grouping(s), and the production of a new epistemology that will replace forms of knowing that are dependent upon heterosexism.

For Sheila Jeffreys, too, 'the institution of heterosexuality' functions effectively in a biological determinist fashion. She would not put it quite like this; rather she describes it as a 'political institution' created and sustained by a number of disparate discourses, for example, that of the sexologists at one extreme, the Marriage Guidance Council in post-war Britain and the 1960s sexual revolutionaries at another.[8] However, the effect, according to her, of these discourses is to create heterosexuality as a biological given. True feminists, for her, therefore, must actively choose to transcend their biology; they must (if necessary) refuse their desires and make the political choice of lesbianism.

The objections of these two constructivists – Wittig and Jeffreys – to the form of biological determinism in question here, are akin to the aforementioned difficulties with the more general type of biological determinism. Either desire is effectively reduced to heterosexual desire, or the latter is foundational for any other type of desire. This idea of a foundation, anyway, constructivists argue, is misleading in so far as no biological phenomenon can be described in terms which make no reference to social or experiential terms.

Extending this, there is a further type of constructivist critique of biological determinism. Some feminists, recently, have expressed considerable interest in 'the body and its desires'. They would argue, however, that no aspect of a person's make-up – her instincts, desires and wishes through to her beliefs – can be regarded as immune from social and cultural conditioning. These feminists would not so much reject biology as argue that its content is socially constructed.

Constructivisms

One form of constructivism about sexuality is the view that one's sexuality is a matter of conscious political choice: Sheila Jeffreys, for example, argues that we can make a conscious choice to give up a particular sexual identity, choice of sexual object or set of sexual desires. A more common approach of sexual constructivists, however, is to see both sexual identity and sexual desire as 'product[s] of social and historical forces'.[9] Sexuality for Weeks is a 'fictional unity' that once did not exist and at some time in the future may not exist again. Weeks is critical of the 'essentialist' approach to sex, and argues that existing languages of sex set the horizon of the possible; there are, he argues, vast ranges and types of sexualities and no certainties about the matter.

Weeks has done an enormous amount of historical research in support of his position. He demonstrates the multiplicity of sexualities, from variations in the form taken by the kinship taboo – 'in the Christian traditions of the Middle Ages', for example, 'marriage to the 7th degree of relationships was prohibited ... In the Egypt of the Pharaohs, sibling marriages were permitted' – to the varying patterns of family life.[10] He quotes Freud: 'The most striking difference between the erotic life of antiquity and our own no doubt lies in the fact that the ancients laid the stress upon the instinct itself, whereas we emphasise its object.'

The prime progenitor, as I pointed out earlier, for many, of recent sexual constructivisms, is Foucault. Sex and sexualities are, for him, the forms of one of the knowledge-power couplets; sexualities proliferated from the seventeenth century on as discourses – Catholicism, medicine, psychiatry, etc. Discourses of sexuality might take on the character of, for instance, 'the internal discourse of the eighteenth century school' – its architectural layout, the rules for monitoring bedtime and sleep periods, the planning of the recreation lessons, or more obvious forms, like the speech of educators, physicians, parents about, for instance, children's sex.[11] But whatever the form they have taken, discourses on sexuality have flourished. Sex, Foucault says, 'became transformed into discourse'.

The discourses of sexuality, according to common readings of Foucault, are one particularly crucial set of exemplifications of the 'regimes of truth' that he seeks to unmask. Medicine, for example, purports to reveal 'the truth' about people's sexualities. In fact, Foucault argues, this commitment to 'the truth' is itself the crucial manifestation of power. The 'science' of medicine creates forms of oppression – the 'pervert', the pederast. The discourses on sexuality construct the subject of sexual desire. 'The subject is not the *vis-à-vis* of power but one of its prime effects.'[12] A person's constitution as a subject is inseparable from her subjection to the power of a 'great interpreter' who is assumed to have privileged access to the truth. In the Catholic confessional, for example, the individual – via the mediation of the priest – ('the interpreter') constructs himself/herself as a sexed being. The sexed subject, then, is subjugated in two senses: in the sense that she/he is 'subject to another by control' and in that she is 'tied to her own identity by consequence of self-knowledge'.

As many commentators have pointed out, Foucault is less interested in revealing some fundamental truth about heterosexual behaviour than in describing how the subject is constructed and controlled through the multifarious discourses on sexuality. For example, demography serves the scientific purpose of achieving population control; psychology, sexology, psychoanalysis – the key 'modern' discourses on sexuality – each seek to locate some fundamental truth about the individual as revealed in her/his sexual behaviour.

Another constructivist, Lacan, analyses sexual drives as mediated through language and linguistic processes.[13] Sexual drives are not 'real', biologically determined or natural; rather they are functions of the effect of the field of the other. The biological 'stages' in the development of sexuality, described by Freud, must be understood, for Lacan, to be mediated by the particular socio-cultural settings in which the child finds him/herself. Sexual desire, like any other form of desire, requires the 'symbolic' for its expression. The Lacanian 'symbolic' places human beings in relation to others. Outside the Lacanian symbolic is psychosis.

Of course, there are vast differences between these various 'constructivisms'. All of them are postmodernist, however, to the extent of emphasising the diversity of sexualities, and most of them, I would argue, have downplayed the role of the biological in sexuality. I believe that one can, contrary to their arguments, however, adopt an 'essentialist' approach to sexuality, whilst accepting the kinds of criticism of 'biological determinist' approaches outlined above.

Constructivisms: A Critique

A weak case can be made against these constructivisms that there is a biological, perhaps even a chemical aspect to sexual desire which renders questionable both the existential notion of 'choice' and the view that this desire is wholly 'created' by social processes. One point is that the human species as a whole – until *in vitro* fertilisation becomes the norm – might be said to need the expression of a heterosexual 'sex drive' if it is to survive. There is, therefore, a species-specific drive which is biologically based. The notion of a species-specific drive need not imply that it is necessarily manifested in the same way in all members of the species. If there were no such drive, then there would be no biological imperative towards the survival of the species, which would be contrary to Darwinian assumptions. Secondly, all human beings are born, as the 'biological' Freud emphasised, with certain instincts or drives that seek release. At least some of these are sexual in character. The drives are both partly biological and universal to the human species. The 'hydraulic' model of sexuality is both plausible to a certain degree, and corroborated by the behaviour of babies and young children.

A further point that can be made is that sexual constructivists tend to see sexuality and sexualities as too malleable. Human bodies, for some, are in danger of slipping altogether out of the picture. On one reading of Jeffreys, as we have seen, sexuality becomes a matter of free will, of free choice. The human being, for her, is ultimately the *homo economicus* of liberal contract theory: there are no sexed bodily human beings interacting with one another; there are only free floating wills, taking on sexual identities and sexual desires as they wish. But there is a tendency for less radical sexual constructivists to share this perspective. For they assume that human nature is plastic and mouldable. Liberal social constructivist environmentalists castigate as 'biological determinism or essentialism' any assumption that human beings have natures or bodily drives (including sex drives). 'Sexuality socialisation theory' relies on a picture of human beings as blank slates or pieces of putty. Sexualities are donned under the influence of prevalent discourses – Roman Catholicism, etc. – and reinforced, like patterns of behaviour. Any differences between people – for instance, differences in gender and sexual orientation – are said to be due to culture and conditioning, and are thought to be eliminable by changing the force of present social conditioning. The argument that sexual reproduction, sexual response and sexual identity are malleable and environmentally created and that the only alternative is a kind of biological determinism is a version of the classic distinction between 'pure freedom' and 'total determinism' or that between 'reason and passion'. There are plenty of examples of these dualisms in operation in sexual constructivists' writings: Plummer, for instance, contrasts the 'drive-based sexologic'[14] with a 'social constructivist' position, whereby sexuality is akin to a 'learned script'; another constructivist, Hastrup, in analysing the concepts of virginity and abortion, contrasts the limited role of physiological realities with multiple social and symbolic meanings.[15] Weeks posits a similar dualism in his division between 'biological essentialism' and 'social constructivism'.

One problem with these dualisms, as many feminists have pointed out, is that they have tended to be associated, in the history of western philosophy, with other dualisms – like that between 'mind' and 'body' – which privilege one side of the divide over the other. To emphasise the mind/reason/freedom aspect of the duality, as do some sexual constructivists, is to reinforce this privileging of the mental over the bodily aspect of the self, and to contribute to the undermining of the domain – the 'natural' realm – which has traditionally been associated with the feminine. Until the seventeenth century, in western thought, the conception of nature as living and material, was commonplace.

Foucault: Constructivist?

I suggested earlier (pp. 133–4) that Foucault is a constructivist. Some people, however, might question this, given his emphasis on the body. Indeed, some critics of Foucault have described as unacceptable what they see as his one-dimensional account of the self as a passive, docile body; his denial of the capacity for rational and autonomous thought. Rorty sees him as taking on an irresponsible 'anarchic Nietzscheanism'.[16] Ian Wright views Foucault's thought as a 'counsel of despair' which rejects any idea of progress in history.[17] On this reading of Foucault, he is the prime progenitor of anti-Enlightenment thinking; he sets out to counterpose the idea of the body to the Enlightenment rational, self-reflective subject and to privilege the emotions, the passions and needs over rational thought. Foucault, in his extensive investigation of bodies and their pleasures, exposes, as Nancy Fraser has put it: 'the undue privilege modern Western culture has accorded subjectivity, sublimation, ideality and the like'.[18] Foucault, throughout his writings, analyses the operations of the multifarious discourses of power – the dominant theorisations of punishment, madness and sexuality – on the body. It is this aspect of Foucault's work which has been vital for feminism. His insistence on the body as an historical and culturally specific entity has been enormously significant for feminism. One of the ways, many feminists argue, in which his thought has been significant for feminism is in its conceiving of the body as a concrete, material phenomenon without reducing this materiality to a fixed biological essence. Some notion of the body, it has been argued, is central to analysis of the oppression of women, because it is upon the biological distinction of the sexes that gender inequality has come about.[19]

I would argue, however, that Foucault's work can be read as accentuating dualism. On the one hand, it can be read this way because it adds the domain of the sexual – the emotions and desires – to the 'discursive' or 'mentalistic' realm. Sexualities are analysed by Foucault, both archaeologically and genealogically, primarily in terms of power relations of domination. The modern subject is constituted as object of knowledge partially through these discourses. Whilst, in one sense, this undercuts the Cartesian dualism of reason/desire, or mind and body, in another sense it reinforces it by contributing to the downgrading of the biological and the natural domain. The emotional is reclassified as socially constructed and rational, in this sense: it is the effect of 'discursive' forces – Christianity, classical Greek thinking – that have been socially and culturally created. In another sense, Foucault's work has been criticised for underplaying the rational dimension – the realm of the individual rational agent who is capable of responding to and resisting those dominant cultural forces. But the latter, important point, does not undermine the claim that he is also emphasising a rational dimension of desire which, in a sense, plays into the hands of a kind of dualism.

I would argue that pre-constructivist writing about sexuality needs to be reanalysed, not as many recent writers have done to demonstrate its heavily constructed character, but to point out the effect of one dimension of it as a 'natural' phenomenon.

This dimension emerges from a look at Plato's *Symposium*.

Sexuality: Another View

In his *Symposium*, Plato presents a view of the nature of love.[20] He models an account of the human experience of love on homoerotic desire. This desire is an experience of 'spiritual' intercourse; indeed, the ultimate 'non-earthly' object of love – the love of beauty – is revealed through it. Plato has been blamed for a spirituality which reduces everyday objects of love to a means to an end, or allows them to be loved only as symbols of a higher reality.[21] There is something in this claim, and it is undoubtedly true that the dualism to which I objected earlier is present in Plato (it is instigated by him after all) and yet there are insights in Plato's writing on love which provide a powerful antidote to the constructivists' picture.

Plato presents a picture of a relationship between an adolescent boy and an older man which is intense, sentimental and unconsummated. Phaedrus, the first spokesperson, presents the idea that love is a sort of frenzy. This is a constant theme in the text: love is manic, irrational, potentially destructive. A person in love – and all loves involve desire and passion – is the opposite of the Stoic ideal of calm self-sufficiency. Love's irrationality, indeed, leads ultimately to death. Many cultural myths – Romeo and Juliet; Abelard and Heloise; Bonnie and Clyde – have played upon this theme. Many writers, too, from de Sade through Freud to Bataille emphasise the connection between eroticism and death. De Sade removes all 'others' in his pursuit of the limits of sexual desire. As Bataille puts it: de Sade 'makes his heroes uniquely self-centred, the partners are denied any rights at all; this is the key to his system'.[22] Many writers have emphasised how when we fall in love, or when we desire another, we experience a loss of control, a sense of helplessness, an inability to make clear, rational decisions. Falling in love, as one writer put it: 'Is individualistic, objectifying, linked to escapist notions of romantic love'.[23] The overwhelming feeling when 'in love' is of intense, uncontrollable emotion.

Aristophanes, another of Plato's spokespeople in the *Symposium*, reaches Phaedrus' conclusion. He recounts how, originally, human beings were spherical objects, which were subsequently split in two, leaving each half to seek out its other. This pursuit is love, which is therefore a form of nostalgia.

For Socrates, however, love does not lead to death, rather it moves one on. Love as a kind of desire implies deficiency: what one loves, one desires, and what one desires, one lacks. Desire, therefore, is always unfulfilled; sentimental, unconsummated homosexual attachments provide the ideal image of the perpetual yearning that he describes.

In the *Symposium*, there is an 'ascent' of loves, which parallels the 'growth' of the mind in the cave and line metaphors in the *Republic*.

> The man who would pursue the right way to this goal must begin, when he is young, by applying himself to the contemplation of physical beauty, and, if he is properly directed by his guide, he will first fall in love with one particular beautiful person. . . . Later he will observe that physical beauty in any person is closely akin to physical beauty in any other and that, if he is to make beauty of outward form the object of his quest, it is great folly not to acknowledge that the beauty exhibited in all bodies is one and the same; when he has reached this conclusion, he will be a lover of all physical beauty. . . . The next stage is for him to reckon beauty of soul more valuable than beauty of body; . . . The man who has been guided thus far in the mysteries of love . . . will suddenly have revealed to him . . . a beauty whose nature is marvellous indeed.[24]

Love, for Plato, is what life is all about, because life is a drama of escape from the gross, transient and illusory existence to a domain of truth, beauty and permanence.

Plato does not really explain how the steps up the rungs of the ladder to appreciation of absolute beauty take place. And this aspect of his theory need not detain us here. Other parts of his theory are important for present purposes. One is his emphasis on the madness, the frenzy of sexual desire. This focus is borne out by much writing on the subject.

The Platonic reading of sexual desire brings to light some limitations of one type of 'constructivism' about sexuality. Even if sexual identity can be willed, sexual desires cannot. Sexual desires cannot be willed or chosen because, by their very nature, they lie partly outside the domain of will and conscious control. This does not necessarily place them, Cartesian fashion, on the 'outside' of reason, in the domain of madness (see Rosi Braidotti for readings of madness in Foucault, Lacan and Descartes as reason's 'other'), because actual desire never involves the total loss of control, the complete suppression of rational faculties.[25] For the other side of love, as Plato puts it, is its ability to move one on, to transcend the limitations of the present. Desire can neither be a product of conscious will nor of social and historical forces. The unconscious, irrational side to it means that it often manifests itself in ways that run contrary to these 'social and historical forces'. It is often out of tune with the person's rationally held beliefs, and with the 'discourses', including the 'bodily discourses', in which the individual is intertwined. It may, indeed, undermine these beliefs and these discourses. Sexual desire may be closer to the Reichean 'involuntary pleasurable contractions' than to the effect of discourses of power.

Foucault recognises this side to sexuality, yet, at times, he appears to want to reject it as an 'inferior', rather 'dirty' form of sexuality. In the discussion with Sennett, *Sexuality and Solitude*, he quotes Augustine as saying (in *The City of God*) that in 'the sexual act', the body is shaken by terrible jerks, and one loses control of oneself. He says:

> The surprising point is not that Augustine would give such a classical description of the sexual act, but the fact that, having made such a horrible description, he then admits that sexual relations could have taken place in Paradise before the Fall.[26]

The rationalist version of control seems strongly to influence Foucault. 'Sex in erection', according to Foucault, 'is the image of men revolted against God. The arrogance of sex is the punishment and consequence of the arrogance of man.'[27] The 'problem' of sexuality becomes, for Christians (and for Foucault, too, it appears), the problem of the relationship between one's 'will and involuntary assertions'.[28] The question of sexual desire becomes part of the will itself. It appears to be treated as a mental phenomenon. Sexuality becomes curiously disembodied, disconnected from the lived experiences of men and women.

Yet, once again, it may be said, there is another reading of Foucault which may be compatible with my argument. Maureen Cain has pointed, recently, to the operation of an 'extra-discursive' domain in Foucault. She refers to Foucault's text 'I, Pierre Rivière, Having Slaughtered my Mother'. She suggests that, although the 'battle among discourses and through discourses' is dominant in the text, underneath them all is 'the parricide with the reddish brown eyes'.[29] Cain discusses several senses of 'extra-discursive' domains – repressed knowledges and unthinkable or unformulated experiences – that operate in Foucault. Sexuality, in my Platonic sense, could form part of this extra-discursive domain. In the 'History of Sexuality', Foucault describes the power–knowledge relations that construct sexuality, in particular historical contexts, as a source of truth. On the other hand, there is, in his work, an alternative view, which allows for the kinds of point I am making. He suggests that bodies and pleasures might be a source of resistance to the hegemonic truth of sexuality.

'Socialisation' is never complete, because competing interests create conflicts. In arbitrating between these interests, there is scope for a kind of 'agency' that might form new interests/desires.

Sexual desire, I am arguing, then, may be liberating because it may unblock the hold of 'repressive' socio-cultural norms. In the social domain, in the 1960s, the 'sexual liberation movement' functioned to reveal politically repressive aspects of the family, of some aspects of state policy, etc. Those who have assumed lesbian or gay identities have helped dispel any cultural norm that relies on the 'naturalness' of heterosexuality. At a purely individual level, allowing free expression to sexual desire may function to 'free' the person from beliefs that may actually have had a constraining effect. In psychoanalysis, sexual emotions may be brought to the surface and allowed expression, and then the 'patient' may be helped to overcome difficulties in life. Foucault, as we know, regarded psychoanalysis as part of the problem: in psychoanalysis, he argued, the individual is 'defined' by reference to her sexual behaviour. This, indeed, if it is true (and there may be some truth in the claim), is a limitation of the 'discourse'; however, it is not true, as Foucault seems to imply, that psychoanalysis cannot help to modify beliefs and real experiences that may be disabling the individual.

Sexuality could be liberating. Women collectively produce, for example, perspectives on sexuality which do not collaborate in the sexist assumption (implicit certainly in Lacanian thought) that the power of the penis/phallus is incontrovertible and monolithic. Women can give expression to fantasies and desires that may contradict or subvert 'patrocentric' or heterosexist norms. Women's sexualities, then, can function as sites of resistance to 'discursively defined' patrocentric sexuality. The same might be true of lesbian sexuality and of the sexuality of any grouping that has been characterised as 'deviant' in respect of some norm. Of course, the other side of the coin is that sexualities, understood this way, as pre-discursive, may also be oppressive. Some men will subjugate and even be violent towards women (or men) if they are allowed the free expression of their desires; some women may find themselves, as a result of the experience of violent subjection, unable to express their desires. This point illustrates, however, not that we need to return to a perspective which has sexualities discursively constructed. Rather it suggests that the form taken by sexual desires is deep-seated and deep-rooted in the individual psyche, and it may require years of painful unravelling of deep-seated unconscious memories, on the part of some women, in order for them to experience desire as liberating. Sexual desire, then, will take the form it does as a result of a combination of the nature of the particular body experiencing the desire and the character of the early Oedipal experiences in which that person was involved, together with other powerfully felt experiences in later life.

There are unconscious and irrational elements to sexual love and desire which are downplayed by the too 'rational' model of the 'social constructivists'. A person's sexual identity is no more created by 'discourses': Catholicism, medicine, etc., than rapists are 'created' by porn. The core of this identity, I would argue, is created by the very powerful influences of early childhood desire. Sexual desires, predilections and fantasies subvert and often contradict social realities and rationally accepted values. Many a feminist – who pours scorn on the adoption of any kind of masochistic role for herself in sexual or other relations with people – fantasises her lover dominating her/beating her, in order to heighten her arousal. The sorts of desire I am now describing can contradict accepted social norms and cannot, therefore, be the creations of them. Far from being the creatures of particular Foucauldian discourses of power, they are much more akin to the Reichian natural or involuntary pleasurable contractions or the Freudian drives or energy seeking release.

The 'social constructivist' picture of sexuality connects readily with a negative view of sources of erotic fantasy such as pornography. It paints a picture of sexuality as malleable, permeable, pliable, subject to manipulation by the conscious self (Jeffreys) or by social forces (Weeks and Foucault). The sexed self is viewed as akin to a social role, that can be donned or removed either at will (Jeffreys) or by appropriate conditioning (Weeks and Foucault). In this sense, it is allied with certain feminist attempts to suppress outlets – like porn – for the enhancement or expression of sexual fantasies. Such feminists believe that rapists are created and moulded by pornographic imagery; that pornography plays a major role in the legitimising of these sorts of sexual acts. I would argue, on the contrary, that the desire on the part of a man to rape a woman is much more likely to have a complex set of causes – some unconscious; some conscious. Rapists will not disappear with the eradication of pornography any more than necrophiliacs or practitioners of sadomasochism would be eliminated were we to do away with Catholicism, medicine or psychiatry. Weeks and Foucault make a very important point: namely that the presence of certain social forms and 'discourses' – like psychiatry – legitimises discrimination against particular groups of people: not only homosexuals. But this point can be made without the much stronger claim that sexual desires and identities are created by these social forms.

Concluding Remarks

This book represents a contribution to debates on feminism and post-modernism. Some of it is introductory, in the hope that it will render some of the more abstruse work in the debates a little more comprehensible to students of the subject. Furthermore, the book's domain has largely been philosophical: it has been concerned with theories of the self, epistemology, ethics and language. In each of the areas on which it touches, there is, of course, a lot more to say. In epistemology, some excellent work is being conducted at the moment, and I refer the reader particularly to an edited collection by Kathleen Lennon and Margaret Whitford, which is coming out of the presses as I write this.[1] In ethics, there is much that has been done and much still to do, reworking some of the key concepts of the liberal humanist tradition. My Chapters 4 and 7 only scratch the surface of debates that are rethinking the role of the biological domain, and of the body in philosophical debates: here I refer to a book that is, again, due to be published as I write, by Elizabeth Grosz: *Volatile Bodies*.[2]

Chapter 8 of the book, on sexuality, is less philosophical than the rest of the book. As I explained, I included this chapter because sexuality has been such a pivotal area for feminists in debates about the fundamental causes of oppression. Many radical feminists in the eighties moved from the early second wave feminist focus on the economic, the social and the political dimensions of women's oppression to look for some more fundamental cross-cultural arena of difference. Writers like Andrea Dworkin and Katherine Mackinnon pointed to the sexualising of women's bodies in representations like pornography as constituting the key causative factor in areas of oppression such as sexual abuse of women and children. Representations of sexuality, they argue, – Mackinnon's book *Only Words* is just out in the UK – constitute, in themselves, one form of action which serves constantly to undermine women.[3]

Many postmodernists object to this conflation of fantasy representation with reality, and to the uniform account of women's oppression these writers present. I have argued, however, that there is a postmodern dimension to the Dworkin/Mackinnon argument, in that it assumes that sexualities can be manipulated and moulded by pornography and other imagery. I have argued against this, in 'modernist' vein, that sexualities and sexual fantasies are more deep-seated than this: sexual fantasies may contradict and subvert accepted social norms and values.

Chapter 8, then, lies outside the more broadly philosophical framework of the rest of the book. It is the only one that does this, however, and I recognise that there are a vast number of areas of debate on feminism and postmodernism: in political and social theory, for example, and in literary theory, which the book does not touch on.

It is my hope, however, that the book may provide some insights for those working in related fields, and some small inspiration to those women to go on to do more of the work that, I believe, needs to be done, to restore a little of the emancipatory hopes some of us had in the seventies. To return to the words of the Introduction, a return cannot and must not be a revival of the old. We are now living in radically different social, economic and political times from the seventies. Postmodernists made us aware of differences – in race, culture and sexual orientation – that we understood, in the seventies, only in very limited and untheorised ways. But many erstwhile feminist activists of the seventies bemoan the loss of vision that radical hopefuls had then. I can only hope that some small strands in this book might set someone else thinking about ways of beginning to restore that vision in the much more fragmented context of the nineties. Lyotard has described the contemporary demise of the 'emancipatory metanarrative'.[4] Another way of viewing this very same phenomenon, however, might be to suggest that the scope for knowledge creation has been increased. Many more people, in the nineties, have the potential to gain access to high level knowledges. Many more people than was the case in the seventies can now gain degree level qualifications. Rather than this tending to produce a fragmentation of 'knowledges', it has the potential to lead in precisely the opposite direction: towards the creation of a more widely held emancipatory vision. The hope would be that as more people from previously dispossessed groupings gain access to high level knowledges, those very people can begin to challenge the link between knowledge and power that Lyotard has described. My hope, then, is that we will begin to see a post-postmodern modernism in feminism.

Notes

Introduction

1. Ihab Hassan, *The Postmodern Turn*, Ohio University Press, Ohio, 1987, p. xi, quoted in A. Callinicos, *Against Postmodernism: A Marxist Critique*, Polity Press, Cambridge, 1989.

2. C. Jencks, *What is Postmodernism?*, Academy, London, 1986, p. 14.

3. J. F. Lyotard, *The Postmodern Condition*, Manchester University Press, Manchester, 1979, p. 80; F. Jameson, *Fables of Aggression*, University of California Press, Berkeley, 1979, p. 2.

4. Andreas Huyssen, 'Mapping the Postmodern', in *Feminism/Postmodernism*, ed. Linda J. Nicholson, Routledge, London and New York, 1990, p. 236.

5. Ibid., p. 244.

6. Peter Burger, *Theory of the Avantgarde*, University of Minneapolis Press, Minneapolis, 1984.

7. Huyssen, 'Mapping the Postmodern', p. 246.

8. Ibid.

9. Ibid.

10. Arthur Kroker and David Cooke, *The Postmodern Scene*, 2nd edition, St Martin's Press, New York, 1986, p. 8.

11. Leslie Fiedler, 'Cross the Border – Close the Gap', in *Postmodernism: A Reader*, ed. Patricia Waugh, Hodder and Stoughton, London, 1992, p. 33.

12. Ibid., p. 25.

13. J. F. Lyotard, 'Defining the Postmodern', ICA Documents 4, 1985, p. 6.

14. P. Waugh, 'Introduction', in *Postmodernism: A Reader*, ed. P. Waugh, Hodder and Stoughton, London, 1992.

15. Jane Flax, *Psychology, Feminism and Postmodernism in the Contemporary West*, University of California Press, Berkeley, 1990, pp. 32–34.

16. Kate Soper, 'Feminism as Critique', *New Left Review*, no. 176, July/Aug. 1989, pp. 91–112.

17. J. Squires (ed.) *Principled Positions, Postmodernism and the Rediscovery of Value*, Lawrence and Wishart, London, 1993, p. 1. See also S. Lovibond, 'Feminism and Postmodernism', *New Left Review*, no. 178, Nov./Dec. 1989, pp. 5–28; Michelle Barrett and Anne Phillips (eds) *Destabilising Theory: Contemporary Feminist Debates*, Polity Press, Cambridge, 1992, p. 6; Susan Bordo, 'Feminism, Postmodernism and Gender Scepticism' and Christine di Stefano, 'Dilemmas of Difference: Feminism, Modernity and Postmodernism', both in *Feminism/Postmodernism*, ed. Linda J. Nicholson, Routledge, London and New York, 1990.

18. Barrett and Phillips, *Destabilising Theory*, p. 6.

19. Squires, *Principled Positions*, p. 2.

20. Patricia Waugh, 'Postmodern Theory: the Current Debate', in *Postmodernism: A Reader*, ed. P. Waugh, Hodder and Stoughton, London, 1992, p. 190.

21. M. Foucault, 'What is Enlightenment?', in *The Foucault Reader*, ed. P. Robinson, trans. C. Porter, Penguin, Harmondsworth, 1984.

1 The Flight from Universals

1. David Hume, *A Treatise of Human Nature*, ed. A. Selby-Bigge, Clarendon Press, Oxford, 1968.

2. Judith Butler, *Gender Trouble, Feminism and the Subversion of Identity*, Routledge, London and New York, 1990.

3. M. Foucault, *Power/Knowledge*, Brighton, The Harvester Press, 1980, pp. 73–74.

4. Ibid., p. 98.

5. A. Assiter, *Althusser and Feminism*, Pluto Press, London, 1990.

6. See Alex Callinicos, *Against Postmodernism: A Marxist Critique*, Polity Press, Cambridge, 1989.

7. S. Freud, 'Mourning and Melancholia', in S. Freud, *On Metapsychology*, Penguin, Harmondsworth, 1984, pp. 251–268.

8. S. Freud, 'The Ego and the Id', in ibid., pp. 351–401.

9. S. Freud, *Three Essays on Sexuality*, trans. James Strachey, Basic Books, New York, 1975.

10. N. Fraser and L. J. Nicholson, 'Social Criticism without Philosophy', in *Feminism/Postmodernism*, ed. L. J. Nicholson, Routledge, London and New York, 1990, pp. 19–38.

11. S. Bordo, who goes on to disgree with her, quoting 'a historian': 'Feminism, Postmodernism and Gender Scepticism', in *Feminism/Postmodernism*, ed. L. J. Nicholson, Routledge, London and New York, 1990, p. 133.

12. J. F. Lyotard, *The Postmodern Condition*, Manchester University Press, Manchester, 1979.

13. R. Rorty, 'Habermas and Lyotard on Modernity', in *Habermas and Modernity*, ed. R. Bernstein, Polity Press, Cambridge, 1985, p. 163.

14. See, for example, Paul Davies, *The Search for a Grand Unified Theory of Nature*, Heinemann, London, 1984.

15. I am indebted for this argument to Gerard O'Donoghue, *Jean François Lyotard and the Postmodern Condition*, a dissertation submitted for the BA Humanities, Brighton University, 1994.

16. P. Feyerabend, *Against Method*, NLB, London, 1975, p. 23.

17. P. Feyerabend, 'Against Method', in *Minnesota Studies in the Philosophy of Science*, vol. IV, University of Minnesota Press, Minneapolis, 1970, p. 84.

18. P. Feyerabend, 'How to be a good Empiricist – A Plea for Tolerance in Matters Epistemological', in *Readings in the Philosophy of Science*, ed. B. A. Brody, Prentice Hall, New Jersey, 1970, p. 326.

19. See Margaret Whitford, *Luce Irigaray: Philosophy in the Feminine*, Routledge, London, 1991, p. 5.

20. Hilary Putnam, *Mind, Language and Reality*, Cambridge University Press, Cambridge, 1975.

21. Fraser and Nicholson, 'Social Criticism without Philosophy', p. 27.

22. L. Segal, *Is the Future Female?* Virago, London, 1987, pp. 213 and 214.

23. J. Martin, 'Methodological Essentialism, False Difference and other Dangerous Traps', University of Chicago Press, *Signs*, vol. 19, no. 2, spring 1994.

24. S. Firestone, *The Dialectic of Sex: The Case for Feminist Revolution*, Paladin, London, 1971, p. 15.

25. Ibid., p. 16.

26. Ibid., p. 17.

27. Ibid., p. 20.

28. Ibid., p. 188.

29. Ibid., p. 191.

30. W. Seccombe, 'The Housewife and her Labour under Capitalism', *New Left Review*, no. 83, 1978, and J. Gardiner, 'Women's Domestic Labour', *New Left Review*, no. 89, 1975.

31. See Betty Friedan, *The Feminine Mystique*, Norton, New York, 1963.

32. See Margaret Coulson, Banka Megas and Hilary Wainwright, 'The Housewife and her Labour under Capitalism: A Critique', *New Left Review*, no. 89, 1975.

33. See, for example, Angela Miles, 'Economics and Feminism, Hidden in the Household: A Comment on the Domestic Labour Debate', *Studies in Political Economy*, no. 11, summer 1985.

34. N. Chodorow, *The Reproduction of Mothering: Psychoanalysis and the Sociology of Gender*, University of California Press, Berkeley, 1978.

35. L. Althusser and E. Balibar, *Reading Capital*, NLR, London, 1970, p. 83.

36. Ibid., p. 84.

2 Irigaray, Lacan and Derrida

1. See Janet Sayers, *Biological Politics*, Tavistock, London, 1982, p. 148; Lynne Segal, *Is the Future Female?*, Virago, London, 1987, p. 133; Cora Kaplan, 'Pandora's Box: Subjectivity and Sexuality in Socialist-Feminist Criticism', in *Making a Difference: Feminist Literary Criticism*, ed. Gayle Green and Coppelia Kahn, Methuen, London, 1985, p. 152; and Toril Moi, *Sexual/Textual Politics*, Methuen, London, 1985, pp. 139 and 148. The latter is a more sophisticated account of Irigaray, but she is still labelled 'essentialist'.

2. See, for example, Claire Duchen, 'Women's Difference', in *French Connections: Voices from the Women's Movement in France*, trans. and ed. Claire Duchen, Hutchinson, London, 1987, p. 55.

3. See, for example, Michelle Barrett, 'The Concept of Difference', *Feminist Review*, no. 26, summer 1987; Ann Rosalind Jones, 'French Theories of the Feminine', in *Making a Difference: Feminist Literary Criticism*, ed. Gayle Green and Coppelia Kahn, Methuen, London, 1985; and Jane Gallop, *Feminism and Psychoanalysis*, Macmillan, London, 1982.

4. Margaret Whitford, *Luce Irigaray: Philosophy in the Feminine*, Routledge, London and New York, 1991, p. 67.

5. Luce Irigaray, *Speculum of the Other Woman*, Cornell University Press, Ithaca, 1985.

6. Luce Irigaray, *This Sex which is Not One*, Cornell University Press, Ithaca, 1985.

7. Ibid., pp. 155–156.

8. Gallop, *Feminism and Psychoanalysis*, p. 74.

9. Irigaray, *This Sex which is Not One*, p. 162.

10. Moi, *Sexual/Textual Politics*, p. 138.

11. Irigaray, *This Sex which is Not One*, p. 74.

12. Jacques Derrida, *Of Grammatology*, Johns Hopkins University Press, Baltimore and London, 1976, p. 162.

13. See, for example, Newton Garver, 'The Philosophy of Jacques Derrida', *Journal of Philosophy*, November 1977.

14. See Jacques Derrida, 'Limited Inc', *Glyph*, 2, 1977, pp. 162–254.

15. Jean Jacques Rousseau, *Essai sur l'origine des Langues*, Bucros, Bordeaux, 1968, Chapter 2.

16. Jean Jacques Rousseau, *The Discourse on the Origin of Inequality*, Everyman, London, 1966, p. 182.

17. Derrida, *Of Grammatology*, p. 173.

18. Ibid.

19. Ibid., p. 182.

20. Jean Jacques Rousseau, *The Confessions*, Book VIII, Penguin, London, 1984, p. 336.

21. Ibid., p. 155.

22. Derrida, *Of Grammatology*, p. 159.

23. Jonathan Culler, *On Deconstruction: Theory and Criticism after Structuralism*, Routledge, London, 1987, p. 104.

24. Jean Jacques Rousseau, quoted in Derrida, *Of Grammatology*, p. 208.

25. Jean Jacques Rousseau, 'Emile', quoted in Derrida, *Of Grammatology*, p. 211.

26. Jacques Lacan, *Ecrits: A Selection*, Tavistock, London, 1977, p. 114.

27. Sigmund Freud, 'Project for a Scientific Psychology', in *The Origin of Psychoanalysis*, ed. M. Bonaparte, A. Freud and E. Kris, Hogarth, London, 1954.

28. Sigmund Freud, 'On Narcissism: An Introduction', SE XIV, 1914, pp. 65–101.

29. Ibid., p. 69.

30. Sigmund Freud, 'The Ego and the Id', SE XIX, 1923, p. 26.

31. Jacques Lacan, 'The Mirror Stage as Formative of the Function of I as Revealed in Psychoanalytic Experience', in *Ecrits: A Selection*, Tavistock, London, 1977.

32. J. W. F. Hegel, *The Phenomenology of Mind*, trans. A. V. Miller, Oxford University Press, Oxford, 1979.

33. Lacan, 'The Mirror Stage', p. 2.

34. Ibid.

35. See, for example, T. Brennan, 'Introduction', *Between Feminism and Psychoanalysis*, ed. T. Brennan, Routledge, London and New York, 1989, p. 2.

36. Jacques Lacan, *Discours de Rome, Le Séminaire Livre III, Les Psychoses*, Paris, 1981, Chapter 14.

37. Lacan, *Ecrits: A Selection*, p. 126.

38. Peter Dews, *The Logics of Disintegration: Post Structuralist Thought and the Claim of Critical Theory*, Verso, London, 1987, p. 84.

39. Ibid.

40. Jacques Lacan, 'La relation d'objet et les structures freudiennes – compte rendu du 4ᵉ séminaire', *Bulletin de Psychologie*, vol. xi, 1957, trans. by Peter Dews in *Logics of Disintegration*, p. 85.

41. E. Grosz, *Jacques Lacan: A Feminist Introduction*, Routledge, London and New York, 1990, p. 104.

42. Carol Williams, 'Feminism, Subjectivity and Psychoanalysis: Towards a Corporeal Knowledge', in *Knowing the Difference: Feminist Perspectives in Epistemology*, ed. Kathleen Lennon and Margaret Whitford, Routledge, London, 1994, p. 170.

43. Luce Irigaray, 'The Poverty of Psychoanalysis', in *The Irigaray Reader*, ed. Margaret Whitford, Blackwell, Oxford, 1991, Chapter 5, p. 84.

44. Jacques Derrida, *Positions*, University of Chicago Press, Chicago, 1981, p. 41.

45. Irigaray, *This Sex which is Not One*, p. 155.

46. Ibid., pp. 155–156.

47. Ibid., p. 74.

48. Ibid., p. 68.

49. Ibid.

50. Moi, *Sexual/Textual Politics*, p. 130.

51. Ibid.

52. Andrea Nye, *Feminist Theory and the Philosophies of Man*, Croom Helm, London, 1988, p. 151.

53. M. Whitford, 'Introduction', *The Irigaray Reader*, Blackwell, Oxford, 1991, p. 8.

54. Irigaray, *Speculum*, p. 183.

55. Ibid.

56. Ibid., p. 191.

57. Ibid.

58. Ibid.

59. Ibid., p. 192.

60. Ibid.

61. Ibid., p. 193.

62. Monique Plaza, 'Phallomorphic Power and the Psychology of Women', *Ideology and Consciousness*, autumn 1978, pp. 4–36.

63. Hélène Cixous, 'Utopias', in *New French Feminisms*, ed. Elaine Marks and Isabelle de Coutivron, Harvester, Brighton, 1980, p. 253.

64. Whitford, *The Irigaray Reader*, p. 9.

65. Irigaray, *This Sex which is Not One*, p. 25.

66. Ibid., pp. 25–26.

67. Ibid., p. 33.

68. Ibid.

69. Nye, *Feminist Theory*, p. 152.

70. Maurice Merleau-Ponty, *The Phenomenology of Perception*, Routledge & Kegan Paul, London, 1962, p. 354.

71. E. Grosz, 'Philosophy, Subjectivity and the Body: Kristeva and Irigaray', in *Feminist Challenges, Social and Political Theory*, ed. Carole Pateman and Elizabeth Grosz, Allen and Unwin, Australia and New Zealand, 1986, pp. 135–136.

72. Shoshana Felman, 'The Critical Phallacy', *Diacritics*, winter 1975, pp. 2–10, quoted in Moi, *Sexual/Textual Politics*, p. 138.

73. Whitford, *The Irigaray Reader*, p. 20.

74. Luce Irigaray, 'Le Langue des Déments', in her *Approaches to Semiotics*, Mouton, The Hague, 1973.

75. Moi, *Sexual/Textual Politics*, p. 147.

76. Ibid.

77. See, for example, S. Harding, *The Science Question in Feminism*, Oxford University Press, Oxford, 1986, Ch. 7.

3 Realism and Anti-Realism

1. J. Koethe, quoting Hilary Putnam, 'Putnam's Argument Against Realism', *Philosophical Review*, vol. lxxxviii, no. 1, Jan. 1979, p. 92.

2. R. Bhaskar, *Reclaiming Reality*, Verso, London, 1989, p. 12.

3. R. Bhaskar, *A Realist Theory of Science*, Leeds Books, Leeds, 1975, p. 22.

4. Richard Rorty, *Philosophy and the Mirror of Nature*, Blackwell, Oxford, 1983, p. 264.

5. Ibid., p. 12.

6. Ibid., p. 259.

7. Ibid., p. 260.

8. Ibid., p. 288.

9. Ibid., p. 293.

10. Bhaskar, *Reclaiming Reality*, p. 205.

11. G. Bachelard, *Le Nouvel Esprit Scientifique*, Presses Universitaires de France, Paris, 1934, pp. 12–13.

12. Koethe, again quoting Putnam, in Koethe, 'Putnam's Argument Against Realism', p. 93. For those who are interested, this argument has been contested. Putnam, though originally a realist, later on has reneged on his realism. He argues as follows: the metaphysical realist requires that an ideal theory – i.e. a deductively closed, consistent set of sentences – on operational criteria may be false. But Putnam now argues that this cannot be. He assumes that the world can be broken into infinitely many pieces: that a theory T1 says that there are infinitely many things. T1 is consistent and has only infinite models. T1 therefore (by the completeness theorem) has a model of every infinite cardinality. He says: choose a model of the same cardinality as the world and map the individuals of the model one-to-one onto the pieces of the world. Using the mapping to define the relation of the model in the world, one gets a satisfaction relation: a 'correspondence' between the terms of the model and sets of pieces of the world, 'such that the theory comes out true – true of the *world* – provided we just interpret 'true' as 'TRUE (SAT)'' (Koethe's italics). Therefore the claim that an 'ideal' theory might be false appears to collapse into unintelligibility.

   But there is a reply to this which is given by Koethe. He gives two arguments against Putnam. The first reply presupposes 'internal realism': that 'earlier theories are, very often, limiting cases of later theories' and that 'theoretical terms (preserve) their reference across most changes of theory.' He suggests we take Tt–1, Tt, and Tt+1 as a temporally ordered succession of non-ideal theories each of which is accepted at the time on the basis of the strictest operational constraints. The referents of all the terms common to the theories are preserved in the transition from one to another. According to the metaphysical realist, Tt, at the time of its acceptance, might be false of the real world. Koethe argues against Putnam that TRUE (SAT) is an acceptable translation of 'true' only if SAT is an acceptable interpretation of 'reference'. Reference, by hypothesis, is preserved from Tt to Tt+1 and the proponents of both Tt and Tt+1 accept it. SAT is defined on the basis of a model of Tt, in which case, if Tt and Tt+1 are inconsistent, Tt+1 must be partially false. So in order for proponents of Tt+1 to accept the interpretation of reference as SAT and hold that reference is preserved in the transition, they would have to hold that Tt+1 is false. But that is contrary to the supposition that they accept Tt+1. Therefore proponents of T1 have a basis for rejecting the interpretation of true as TRUE (SAT) (p. 94).

13. F. de Saussure, *Course in General Linguistics*, ed. C. Bally and A. Sechelieye

in collaboration with A. Riedlinger, McGraw Hill, New York, Toronto, London, 1966.

14. Ibid., p. 88.

15. J. Derrida, *Of Grammatology*, Johns Hopkins University Press, Baltimore and London, 1976, p. 44.

16. Ibid., p. 35.

17. Ibid.

18. Ibid., p. 31.

19. Ibid.

20. Ibid., p. 11.

21. J. Derrida, *Writing and Difference*, Routledge, London, 1981.

22. Ibid., p. 280.

23. Ibid.

24. A. Callinicos, *Against Postmodernism: A Marxism Critique*, Polity Press, Cambridge, 1989, p. 79.

25. J. Derrida, *Glas*, Galilee, Paris, 1974; *Positions*, University of Chicago Press, Chicago, 1981.

26. P. Dews, *The Logics of Disintegration: Post Structuralist Thought and the Claim of Critical Theory*, Verso, London, 1987, p. 70.

27. Ibid.

28. J. Lacan, *Ecrits: A Selection*, Tavistock, London, 1977, pp. 40–113.

29. J. Lacan, *Le Séminaire: Les Ecrits Techniques de Freud*, Paris, 1975, p. 223.

30. Lacan, *Ecrits*, p. 126.

31. Ibid., p. 83.

32. J. Lacan, *Seminaire*, p. 240.

33. Lacan, *Ecrits*, p. 40.

34. Ibid., p. 43.

35. Ibid.

36. L. Irigaray, *This Sex which is Not One*, Cornell University Press, Ithaca, 1985, p. 155.

37. Ibid., pp. 155–156.

38. L. Irigaray, *Speculum of the Other Woman*, Cornell University Press, Ithaca, 1985, p. 21.

39. Irigaray, *This Sex which is Not One*, p. 80.

4 Irigaray and the Self

1. Jacques Derrida, *Margins of Philosophy*, Chicago University Press, Chicago, 1982.

2. Margaret Whitford, *Luce Irigaray: Philosophy in the Feminine*, Routledge, London and New York, 1991, p. 42.

3. Ibid., p. 44.

4. Luce Irigaray, *This Sex which is Not One*, Cornell University Press, Ithaca, 1985, p. 24.

5. Ibid., p. 25.

6. Ibid., p. 26.

7. Ibid., p. 84.

8. Ibid., p. 31.

9. Ibid., Chapter 3.

10. Ibid, p. 39.

11. Rosi Braidotti, *Patterns of Dissonance*, Polity Press, Cambridge, 1991, p. 19.

12. Ibid., p. 104.

13. Irigaray, *This Sex which is Not One*, p. 74.

14. Ibid., p. 120.

15. Luce Irigaray, *Speculum of the Other Woman*, Cornell University Press, Ithaca, 1985, p. 181.

16. Ibid.

17. Ibid., p. 186.

18. See Derek Parfit, *Reasons and Persons*, Clarendon Press, Oxford, 1994, pp. 200–205.

19. Colin McGinn, *The Character of Mind*, 2nd edn, Oxford University Press, Oxford, 1990, p. 109.

20. Godfrey Vesey, *Personal Identity*, Open University, for Course A303 'Problems of Philosophy', Units 5–6, p. 32.

21. Pat Fitzgerald, *Carry on Being: An Investigation into the Continuity of Personal Identity*, dissertation submitted for BA Hons, Brighton Polytechnic, 1992.

22. Sydney Shoemaker, 'Personal Identity', in *Personal Identity*, ed. S. Shoemaker and R. Swinburne, Blackwell, Oxford, 1984, p. 72.

23. Fitzgerald, *Carry on Being*, p. 7.

24. Parfit, *Reasons and Persons*, p. 199.

25. Braidotti, *Patterns of Dissonance*, p. 51.

26. J.-P. Sartre, *Critique of Dialectical Reason*, trans. Alan Sheridan Smith, NLB, London, 1976.

5 Feminist Epistemological Communities

1. Sandra Harding, 'Rethinking Standpoint Epistemology: What is "Strong Objectivity"?' in *Feminist Epistemologies*, ed. Linda Alcoff and Elizabeth Potter, Routledge, London, 1993, pp. 49–83.

2. Alasdair MacIntyre, *Three Rival Versions of Moral Inquiry*, Duckworth, London, 1990.

3. Ibid., p. 60.

4. Anne Seller, 'Towards a Politically Adequate Epistemology', in *Feminist Perspectives in Philosophy*, ed. M. Griffiths and M. Whitford, Macmillan, London, 1988.

5. Lorraine Code, *What Can She Know? Feminist Theory and the Construction of Knowledge*, Cornell University Press, Ithaca and London, 1991.

6. Helen Longino, *Science as Social Knowledge*, Princeton University Press, Princeton, 1990.

7. See, for example, Helen Longino, ibid.; and Lynn Nelson, *Who Knows: From Quine to a Feminist Empiricism*, Temple Press, Philadelphia, 1990.

8. T. Kuhn, *The Structure of Scientific Revolutions*, 2nd edn, University of Chicago Press, Chicago, 1970.

9. Alasdair MacIntyre, *Whose Justice? Which Rationality?*, Duckworth, London, 1988.

10. Ibid., p. 34.

11. Code, *What Can She Know?*

12. Benedict Anderson, *Imagined Communities: Reflections on the Origins and Rise of Nationalism*, Verso, London, 1982.

13. Anne Seller, 'Should the Feminist Philosopher Stay at Home?' in *Knowing the Difference: Feminist Perspectives in Epistemology*, ed. K. Lemon and M. Whitford, Routledge, London, 1994, pp. 230–249.

14. Sandra Harding, *Whose Science, Whose Knowledge? Thinking from Women's Lives*, Oxford University Press, Oxford, 1991.

15. Gayatri Chakravorty Spivak, 'Subaltern Studies: Deconstructing Historiography', in *In Other Worlds: Essays in Cultural Politics*, Routledge, London, 1988.

16. Harding, 'Rethinking Standpoint Epistemology' and *Whose Science, Whose Knowledge*.

17. Ruth Hubbard, 'Have Only Men Evolved?' in *Discovering Reality: Feminist*

Perspectives in Epistemology: Metaphysics, Methodology and the Philosophy of Science, ed. S. Harding and M. Hintikka, D. Reidel, Boston, London and Dordrecht, 1983.

18. See, for example, Carol Gilligan, *In a Different Voice: Psychology and Women's Moral Development*, Harvard University Press, Cambridge, Mass., 1982.

19. Sandra Harding, *The Science Question in Feminism*, Open University Press, Milton Keynes, 1986, p. 72.

20. Jane Flax, 'Gender as a Social Problem: In and for Feminist Theory', *Journal of the American Association for American Studies*, 1986, p. 37, quoted in Harding, *The Science Question*, p. 154.

21. Ibid.

22. Ibid.

23. Harding, *The Science Question*, p. 154.

24. Ibid., p. 165.

25. Ibid., p. 168.

26. Jean Grimshaw, *Feminist Philosophers: Women's Perspectives on Philosophical Traditions*, Wheatsheaf, Brighton, 1986.

27. Harding, 'Rethinking Standpoint Epistemology', p. 60.

28. G. Lukács, *History and Class Consciousness*, Merlin Press, London, 1971.

29. E. Nagel, 'The Absurd', in *Life and Meaning: A Reader*, ed. O. Hanfling, Blackwell, Oxford, 1988, pp. 39–49.

30. Ibid., p. 54.

31. Susan Bordo, 'Feminism, Postmodernism and Gender Scepticism', in *Feminism/Postmodernism*, ed. Linda J. Nicolson, Routledge, London and New York, 1990, p. 145.

32. This expression comes from Seyla Benhabib in 'The Generalised and The Concrete Other', in *Feminism as Critique: Essays on the Politics of Gender in Late Capitalist Societies*, ed. S. Benhabib and Drucilla Cornell, Polity Press, Cambridge, 1987.

33. Spivak, 'Subaltern Studies'.

34. Anderson, *Imagined Communities*.

6 Feminism and Morality

1. G. W. F. Hegel, *The Phenomenology of Spirit*, trans. A. V. Miller, Oxford University Press, Oxford, 1977, pp. 266–290.

2. I. Kant, *Observations on the Feeling of the Beautiful and the Sublime*, trans.

J. T. Goldthwait, University of California Press, Berkeley and Los Angeles, 1960, p. 81.

3. Jean Grimshaw, *Feminist Philosophers: Women's Perspectives on Philosophical Traditions*, Wheatsheaf, Brighton, 1986, pp. 42–43.

4. Carol Gilligan, *In a Different Voice: Psychology and Women's Moral Development*, Harvard University Press, Cambridge, Mass., 1982.

5. N. Fraser and L. J. Nicholson, 'Social Criticism without Philosophy', in *Feminism/Postmodernism*, ed. L. J. Nicholson, Routledge, London and New York, 1990, p. 38.

6. K. Soper, 'Feminism as Critique', *New Left Review*, no. 176, July/Aug. 1989, pp. 91–112.

7. S. Benhabib, 'The Generalised and the Concrete Other: the Kohlberg–Gilligan Controversy and Feminist Theory', in *Feminism as Critique: Essays on the Politics of Gender in Late Capitalist Societies*, ed. S. Benhabib and D. Cornell, Polity Press, Cambridge, 1987.

8. G. Lloyd, *The Man of Reason: 'Male' and 'Female' in Western Philosophy*, Methuen, London, 1984.

9. Miranda Fricker, 'Reason and Emotion', *Radical Philosophy*, No. 57, spring, 1991.

10. F. Jameson, 'Postmodernism, or the Cultural Logic of Late Capitalism', *New Left Review*, no. 146, 1984.

11. P. Waugh, *Postmodernim: A Reader*, Hodder and Stoughton, London, 1992, p. 199.

12. Jessica Benjamin, 'Shame and Sexual Politics', *New German Critique*, no. 27, 1982, pp. 151–159.

13. I. Kant, *Groundwork of the Metaphysic of Morals*, (1785), in *The Moral Law*, ed. H. J. Paton, 3rd edn, Hutchinson, London, 1956.

14. H. Frankfurt, 'Freedom of the Will and the Concept of a Person', *Journal of Philosophy*, vol. 68, 1971, p. 8.

15. M. Foucault, 'What is Enlightenment?', in *The Foucault Reader*, ed. P. Rabinow, Penguin, Harmondsworth, 1984, p. 38.

16. Lois McNay, *Foucault and Feminism*, Polity Press, Cambridge, 1992, p. 85.

17. Ibid., p. 88.

18. Ibid., p. 89.

19. M. Foucault, 'Structuralism and Post Structuralism: An Interview With Michel Foucault', *Telos*, 1983, p. 202, in McNay, *Foucault and Feminism*, Polity Press, Cambridge, 1992, p. 90.

20. J. Rajchman, 'Ethics after Foucault', *Social Text*, vol. 13, 1985, pp. 166–167, in McNay, *Foucault and Feminism*, Polity Press, Cambridge, 1992, p. 91.

21. J. Benjamin, 'Authority and the Family Revisited: Or, a World Without Fathers', *New German Critique*, 1978, p. 51.

22. McNay, *Foucault and Feminism*, p. 101.

23. Pauline Johnson, 'Feminism and Images of Autonomy', *Radical Philosophy*, vol. 40, autumn 1988.

7 Essentialism and Universalism Revisited

1. Christine Delphy, *The Main Enemy*, WRRC, London, 1977.

2. Elizabeth Fee, 'Nineteenth Century Craniology: The Study of the Female Skull', *Bulletin of the History of Medicine*, vol. 53, 1979, pp. 415–433.

3. Herbert Spencer, *The Principles of Biology*, Appleton, New York, 1867, p. 485.

4. Ruth Bleier, *Science and Gender: A Critique of Biology and its Theories on Women*, Pergamon Press, New York, 1984, p. 50.

5. Robert Verrall, 'Sociobiology: The Instincts in our Genes', *Spearhead*, March 1979, p. 8.

6. E. O. Wilson, *On Human Nature*, Wendan, Harvard University Press, Cambridge, Mass., 1978, p. 4.

7. Richard Dawkins, *The Selfish Gene*, Paladin, London, 1985.

8. Wilson, *On Human Nature*, p. 133.

9. Ibid.

10. P. L. Van den Berghe and D. P. Barash, 'Inclusive Fitness and Human Frailty Structure', *American Anthropologist*, no. 79, 1977, pp. 809–823.

11. Bleier, *Science and Gender*, p. 17.

12. Wilson, *On Human Nature*, p. 129.

13. Bleier, *Science and Gender*, p. 23.

14. Donna Haraway, *Private Visions: Gender, Race and Nature in the World of Modern Science*, Routledge, London, 1989, p. 144.

15. A. MacIntyre, 'Ideology, Social Science and Revolution', *Comparative Politics*, no. 5, 1973, pp. 321–342.

16. Anne Oakley, *Sex, Gender and Society*, Temple Smith, London, 1972, p. 158.

17. Michelle Barrett, *Women's Oppression Today: Problems in Marxist Feminist Analysis*, Verso, London, p. 13.

18. Alison Jaggar, *Feminist Politics and Human Nature*, Harvester, Brighton, 1983, p. 28.

19. Moira Gatens, 'A Critique of the Sex–Gender Distinction', in *A Reader in Feminist Knowledge*, ed. Sneja Gunew, Routledge, London and New York, 1991, p. 140.

20. Simone de Beauvoir, *The Second Sex*, Penguin, Harmondsworth, 1975, p. 189.

21. Ibid., p. 406.

22. Ibid, pp. 406–407.

23. Ibid., p. 54.

24. Ibid.

25. Ibid., pp. 60–61.

26. Lois McNay, *Foucault and Feminism*, Polity Press, Cambridge, 1992, p. 22.

27. J. Butler, *Gender Trouble, Feminism and the Subversion of Identity*, Routledge, London and New York, 1990, p. 6.

28. R. Stoller, *Sex and Gender: The Development of Masculinity and Femininity*, vol. I, Maresfield Reprints, London, 1984.

29. Ibid., p. 70.

30. Ibid., pp. 24–28.

31. Ibid.

32. Ibid.

33. Val Plumwood, 'The Sex/Gender Distinction', *Radical Philosophy*, no. 51, spring 1989.

34. R. Braidotti, 'The Politics of Ontological Difference', in *Between Feminism and Psychoanalysis*, ed. T. Brennon, Routledge, London, 1989, p. 93.

35. G. Chakravorty Spivak, *In Other Worlds: Essays in Cultural Politics*, Methuen, London, 1987.

8 A Critique of Constructivist Accounts of Sexuality

1. See, for example, K. Plummer, 'Sexual Diversity: A Sociological Perspective', in *The Psychology of Sexual Diversity*, ed. K. Howells, Blackwell, Oxford, 1984, pp. 219–253.

2. W. Reich, *The Function of the Orgasm*, trans. T. P. Wolfe, Farrar, Strauss and Giroux, New York, 1961, p. 79.

3. S. Freud, *Three Essays on Sexuality*, trans. James Strachey, Basic Books, New York, 1975 p. 135.

4. See, for example, J. L'Esperance, 'Doctors and Women in the 19th Century: Sexuality and Role', in *Health Care and Popular Medicine in 19th Century England*, ed. J. Woodward and D. Richards, Croom Helm, London, 1977.

5. J. Weeks, *Sexuality*, Routledge, London, 1986, p. 296.

6. In ibid., p. 299.

7. Monique Wittig, 'The Category of Sex', *Feminist Issues*, 1982, pp. 63–69.

8. Sheila Jeffreys, *Anticlimax*, The Women's Free Press, London, 1989, p. 3.

9. Weeks, *Sexuality*, p. 15.

10. Ibid., p. 27.

11. Michel Foucault, *The History of Sexuality*, vol. 1, *An Introduction*, ed. Robert Hurley, Allen Lane, New York, 1979, p. 28.

12. Ibid., p. 116.

13. See Jacques Lacan, *Ecrits*, trans. Alan Sheridan, W. W. Norton & Co., New York, 1977.

14. Plummer, 'Sexual Diversity'.

15. K. Hastrup, 'The Semantics of Biology: Virginity', in *Defining Females: The Nature of Women in Society*, ed. S. Ardener, John Wiley, New York, 1978, pp. 49–65.

16. Clare O'Farrell, *History or Philosophy*, Macmillan, Basingstoke, repr. 1993, p. 114, quoting R. Rorty, 'Moral Identity and Private Autonomy', paper presented at an international conference, 9–11 January 1988.

17. I. Wright, 'The Suicide of the Intellectuals', *Times Higher Education Supplement*, 24 October 1986.

18. Nancy Fraser, *Unruly Practices: Power, Discourse and Gender in Contemporary Social Theory*, Polity Press, Cambridge, 1989, p. 62.

19. See, for example, S. Blee Bartky, *Femininity and Dementia: Studies in the Phenomenology of Oppression*, Routledge, London, 1990 and Carolien Ramazanoglu, (ed.) *Up Against Foucault: Explorations of some Tensions between Foucault and Feminism*, Routledge, London, 1992.

20. Plato, *Symposium*, trans. W. Hamilton, Penguin, Harmondsworth, 1980.

21. See, for example, Fergus Kerr, 'Charity as Friendship', in *Language, Meaning and God: Essays in Honour of Herbert McCabe*, ed. Brian Davies, Geoffrey Chapman, London, 1987.

22. G. Bataille, *Eroticism*, Marian Boyar, London and New York, 1987, p. 167.

23. Lucy Goodison, 'Really Being in Love Means Wanting to Live in a Different World', in *Sex and Love: New Thoughts on Old Contradictions*, ed. J. Ryan and S. Cartledge, The Women's Press, London, 1983, p. 48.

24. Plato, *Symposium*, p. 93.

25. Rosi Braidotti, *Patterns of Dissonance: A Study of Women in Contemporary Philosophy*, Polity Press, Cambridge, 1991.

26. M. Foucault and R. Sennett, 'Sexuality and Solitude', in *On Signs: A Semiotics Reader*, ed. M. Blonsky, Blackwell, Oxford, 1985.

27. Ibid., p. 176.

28. Ibid.

29. Maureen Cain, 'Foucault, Feminism and Feeling: What Foucault can and cannot contribute to feminist epistemology', in *Up Against Foucault: Explorations of some Tensions between Foucault and Feminism*, ed. Carolien Ramazanoglu, Routledge, London, 1992, p. 85.

Concluding Remarks

1.   Kathleen Lennon and Margaret Whitford (eds), *Knowing the Difference: Feminist Perspectives in Epistemology*, Routledge, London, 1994.

2.   Elizabeth Grosz, *Volatile Bodies*, Pergamon Press, London, 1994.

3.   Andrea Dworkin, *Pornography: Men Possessing Women*, The Women's Press, London, 1981; K. Mackinnon, *Only Words*, Harper Collins, London, 1994.

4.   J. F. Lyotard, *The Postmodern Condition*, Manchester University Press, Manchester, 1979.

Index